Leading with G.R.A.C.E: Building Civil Sports Communities

A Comprehensive Framework for Creating Excellence Through Character in Athletics

By Alva L. Amaker, M.Ed, CAA, CCT

Copyright

Leading with G.R.A.C.E: Building Civil Sports Communities a Comprehensive Framework for Creating Excellence Through Character in Athletics

Copyright © 2025 by Alva L. Amaker, Vigilant AD

All rights reserved. No part of this publication may be reproduced, distributed, or transmitted in any form or by any means, including photocopying, recording, or other electronic or mechanical methods, without the prior written permission of the publisher, except in the case of brief quotations embodied in critical reviews and certain other noncommercial uses permitted by copyright law.

Published by Propriety Publishing

ISBN: 978-1-77334-105-7 eISBN: 978-1-77334-106-4

First Edition: 2025

Printed in the United States of America

DEDICATION

To Victor Thompson and every young athlete who deserves better than toxic traditions disguised as competitive excellence. May your strength inspire transformation that echoes through generations.

FOREWORD

By Dr. Sharon Anderson

Author of *Emotional Civility: The New Standard of Global Success*

It is with great honor that I write the foreword for Alva Amaker's inspiring book, *Leading with G.R.A.C.E.: Building Civil Sports Programs*. From the very first pages, it becomes clear that this is more than a book about sports—it is a call to transform the culture of athletics through the powerful principles of grace, civility, and intentional leadership.

In a world where competition often overshadows character, Alva Amaker reminds us that true leadership is not defined solely by victories on the field, but by the values instilled in those we lead. Her vision of building sports programs anchored in respect, accountability, and compassion is both refreshing and necessary.

As the author of *Emotional Civility: The New Standard of Global Success*, I deeply resonate with Alva Amaker's emphasis on the role civility plays in shaping lasting success. She demonstrates that leading with grace does not diminish competitiveness—it elevates it, by fostering unity, resilience, and the kind of excellence that endures.

This work is essential reading for coaches, athletic directors, educators, and anyone who desires to see sports programs serve as training grounds not only for skilled athletes, but also for responsible citizens and honorable leaders.

Dr. Alva Amaker has written a book that is both timely and timeless. *Leading with G.R.A.C.E.* will challenge, inspire, and equip readers to build programs where dignity and discipline walk hand in hand. It is a gift to the sports world and to the generations of young people whose lives will be shaped by its message.

— Dr. Sharon Anderson
Author of *Emotional Civility: The New Standard of Global Success*

Table of Contents

Introduction: The Crisis in Sports Culture - Why Civility, Why Now?

Chapter 1: Time for Change - The Evidence for Crisis

Chapter 2: Defining Civility in Sports - What Character Looks Like Under Pressure

Chapter 3: Parental Responsibility in Creating Civil Sports Culture

Chapter 4: When Everyone Shares Responsibility - The Broader Ecosystem

Chapter 5: The Business Case for Civility - Culture as Competitive Advantage

Chapter 6: Character Under Fire - When Values Meet Reality

Chapter 7: Building the Framework - Five Principles That Work

Chapter 8: Understanding Where People Stand - The Culture Map

Chapter 9: Assessing Culture - Measuring What Matters

Chapter 10: Building Skills That Last - Character Competencies

Chapter 11: Implementation - Building Your Program

Chapter 12: Sustaining Change - Building Legacy Programs

Conclusion: Your Choice, Your Legacy

About the Author

Citations and References

Introduction: The Crisis in Sports Culture - Why Civility, Why Now?

"The measure of our strength is not just how we compete, but how we carry each other when the whistle stops blowing."

October 3, 2008

The volleyball match had been intense but clean. Our girls fought hard against their cross-town rivals, losing in four sets—nothing unusual for a Thursday night at Freedom High School. The gym was clearing out, families heading to cars, players gathering their gear.

I walked the building as I always did after events, ensuring everyone got out safely. Twenty-five years as an athletic director had taught me that my responsibility didn't end when the scoreboard went dark.

Then I heard the scream.

Outside in the courtyard, seventeen-year-old Victor Thompson lay bleeding on the concrete. He'd been in the stands all night, cheering for our team, one of those students who showed up to support friends even after his practices or workouts. Now he had over 20 stab wounds over the front and back of his torso.

As I knelt beside him, applying pressure to stop the bleeding, frantically seeking to find any lethal wounds, my mind raced through the weeks leading up to this moment. Three different coaches had requested security at games. Three times, the district had said no—budget constraints, they claimed. Not necessary for high school volleyball.

The student who stabbed Victor wasn't some outside threat. He was a Freedom student who'd been hanging around the gym that night, just another face in the crowd until something set him off during the game. Maybe trash talk between students. Maybe Victor looked at him wrong. I never got the full story.

What I got instead was a seventeen-year-old's blood on my hands and the sickening realization that we'd failed to protect the students we were supposed to keep safe.

That night changed everything for me. It shouldn't have taken violence to force my attention to warning signs that had been everywhere: officials quitting faster than we could train them, parents becoming increasingly aggressive at games, students bringing outside conflicts into school events, and the joy being systematically drained from youth sports.

The statistics I would later discover painted a grim picture. According to the U.S. Center for SafeSport, studies show that 40% to 50% of athletes experience some form of abuse[1]. The National Association of Sports Officials reports that officials consistently cite poor sportsmanship from coaches and parents as a primary concern, with parents being identified as the biggest source of problems[2]. These aren't just numbers—they represent real students like Victor, real families torn apart by violence that was entirely preventable.

But Victor's story doesn't end there. Five years later, he would graduate from college with an education degree and return to Freedom as a teacher and assistant coach, telling me, "I want to bring these principles to a new generation of students." That transformation—from victim to advocate—became possible because of what emerged from that terrible night: a systematic approach to building athletic programs where violence becomes unthinkable because you've created something better.

This book introduces that approach through what I now call the G.R.A.C.E framework: **Goodwill, Respect, Accountability, Civility, and Excellence**. It's not perfect, and it's not magic. It's simply a systematic way to build athletic programs where competition serves character development, where mistakes become learning opportunities, and where young people develop into better human beings through sport.

The Evidence is Clear

We're witnessing a cultural crisis in athletics that goes far beyond individual incidents. Recent research paints a sobering picture:

- Youth sports participation declined from 45% in 2008 to 38% in 2018, according to the Aspen Institute[3]
- The NCAA documents that 85% of athletic trainers believe anxiety among student athletes is a serious concern[4]
- Only about half of umpires who complete one year return for a second year, with the five-to-seven year dropout rate at 80%[5]

But here's what those statistics don't capture: the moment a student starts dreading the car ride home because they know they'll get a performance review instead of support. The official who stops working games because they're tired of being screamed at by parents. The athlete who quits not because they don't love the sport, but because they can't handle the toxic environment surrounding it.

Why This Framework Exists

I didn't write this book to add another feel-good sports manual to your shelf. I wrote it because every coach, every athletic director, every parent deserves better tools than what we had in 2008. Because no one should have to learn these lessons the way I did—with a kid bleeding in their arms.

The framework I'm sharing isn't theoretical. It's designed for athletic administrators who understand that culture isn't just about compliance—it's about creating environments where excellence and integrity thrive together.

This book is part narrative, part manual. It's for leaders who dare to ask: What if discipline and compassion weren't at odds? What if we trained for character with the same intensity we train for championships? What if winning and doing right weren't competing values, but complementary ones?

Every chapter includes stories from the field, practical tools you can implement immediately, and reflection questions designed to help you assess your own program's culture. Because this work isn't theoretical—it's deeply personal, intensely practical, and absolutely necessary.

The choice is yours. Accept the toxic traditions because "that's how it's always been done," or choose transformation. The tools exist. The research supports them. Your athletes are counting on your leadership.

Let's get to work.

Chapter 1

Time for Change – The Evidence for Crisis

Stamped in Blood

Three weeks before Victor was stabbed, Coach Marshall came into my office.

"Alva, we need security at volleyball games. The crowds are getting rowdy. Someone's going to get hurt."

He wasn't wrong. Rival schools, teenage emotions, and Thursday-night energy bubbling just under the surface — the math wasn't hard. I submitted the request to district administration the next day.

Denied. Budget constraints. Volleyball doesn't *"typically"* need security.

Two weeks later, Coach Rodriguez reported a parent following a referee to his car, screaming about missed calls. I submitted a second request.

Denied. "Train your staff to handle crowd control."

One week before it happened, I tried again — this time after a fight at another school's homecoming.

Denied. "We'll revisit this during spring budget planning."

Victor nearly died because we were waiting for spring. That's the culture we're fighting: one where violence is predictable, preventable — and still somehow acceptable. Because acknowledging it costs money. Because acknowledging it means admitting we've allowed certain behaviors to become normal.

Three Days Before the Blood

In Conference Room B, under fluorescent lights that buzzed like an accusation, my request sat on the table for the third time in three weeks. District AD Williams didn't look up from his spreadsheet.

"Volleyball?" He finally glanced at me. "Since when does girls' volleyball need security?"

Coach Marshall's warning echoed in my head.

"The energy's been different this season," I said. "Crowds are more aggressive. Parents—"

"Parents have always been passionate."
Stamp.
DENIED.

"We'll revisit in spring budget planning."

Spring.

I thought of Victor Thompson. Seventeen. Loyal. Always in the Freedom football jersey, cheering for teammates he'd known since elementary school.

I should have fought harder.

Three days later, I knelt beside Victor on cold concrete, his blood soaking through my denim shirt. Sirens wailed. His hands shook.

Hope and budget constraints don't stop stab wounds from puncturing teenage dreams.

But back in that conference room, Williams was already back to his numbers, lives reduced to line items. And I gathered my papers and walked out.

I should have fought harder.

The Numbers Can't Scream

The statistics came later — confirming what my hands already knew that night.

- **40–50%** of athletes experience some form of abuse.

- **Officials** quit at rates approaching **80%** after just a few years.

- **Youth sports participation** is dropping — not just due to cost, but because joy has been systematically extracted from the game.

But statistics don't bleed. They don't whisper, *"Ms. Amaker, I don't want to die."*

They don't measure the silence in a locker room where seniors have spent weeks breaking down freshmen. Or the shame of a ref who drives an extra hour just to avoid a school where he's treated like the enemy.

The crisis isn't just in the numbers. It's in the space between them — the stories that don't make it into research papers but live in the hearts of kids who used to love sports... until loving it hurt too much.

This Isn't Isolated. It's Cultural.

This isn't about one school. Or one incident. It's happening everywhere.

- In **Branchburg, New Jersey**, a man broke a 72-year-old umpire's jaw at a youth game. As EMTs arrived, parents shouted that "he deserved it."

- In **Salt Lake City**, **Watsonville**, and **Brooklyn**, youth coaches were arrested for sexual abuse within a five-month span.

- In Canada, **84.5%** of young athletes report experiencing at least one form of violence in sports.

This is not anecdotal. This is structural.

Dr. Chris Stankovich, one of the few people still tracking this over time, put it bluntly:

> "I wish I could report fewer cases of violence and aggression in youth sports, but that simply hasn't happened."

Each week brings a new headline. None of it's surprising anymore.

You Can't Metal Detect a Mindset

After Victor was attacked, everyone suddenly cared about security.
Metal detectors. Bag checks. Chaperones.

But violence doesn't start at the gate. It starts *before* the games — in the stands, locker rooms, and group chats. You can't scan for the attitude that makes violence feel justified.

Schools respond by banning parents instead of educating them. Hiring more security instead of addressing why security became necessary. Writing zero-tolerance policies without building the emotional tools to choose better in the first place.

This is culture triage — not culture change.

If we want violence to become unthinkable, we have to offer something better. And we have to build it before the blood hits the ground.

Everything It Touches

When violence becomes routine, it doesn't stay in the gym.

- **Kids** bring that trauma into their friendships, their classrooms, their families.

- **Officials** walk away, and entire leagues collapse under the weight of not having anyone to call games.

- **Coaches** burn out, not from long hours, but from managing toxic expectations instead of teaching skills.

The costs aren't just financial. They're human. They're spiritual. Every time we ignore this problem, we lose something we can't easily get back.

And eventually, we stop recognizing the games we once believed in.

Not Easier — Just Better

Here's what I've learned since that night:
Crisis can create clarity.

The best programs — the ones that recover and grow — don't wait for policy changes. They build cultures where pressure doesn't become permission for abuse. Where excellence and empathy live in the same huddle. Where competition sharpens character, not breaks it.

This isn't about going soft. It's about going **smart**. And it's about deciding that whatever we're doing now? It's not enough.

But there *is* a better way. We just have to be willing to give up comfort to reach it.

Warnings We Ignored

The warning signs are always there.

- Parents getting angrier, louder.
- Officials quietly turning down assignments.
- Athletes withdrawing from sports they once loved.
- Coaches spending more time putting out fires than building teams.

Programs that stay ahead of the crisis don't ignore these signals — they act. They build culture with the same intensity they build plays. They don't wait for blood to validate what they already know.

Culture isn't an accident. It's built. Or it's allowed to rot.

Reflection Questions

1. **Crisis Recognition:** What specific indicators in your program might signal similar problems? Have you noticed declining referee retention, increasing parent complaints, or athletes quitting mid-season?

2. **Warning Signs Assessment:** Of the warning signs mentioned in this chapter, which ones have you observed in your program or community? How have you responded to them?

3. **System Evaluation:** When problems arise in your program, do your current systems address root causes or just manage symptoms?

4. **Community Impact:** If a serious incident occurred at your event and became public, how would it reflect on your program's preparation and culture?

Chapter Assignment

Conduct a "Culture Vulnerability Assessment" of your current program:

- Survey your officials about their experience working your events
- Review parent complaints from the past two years for patterns
- Interview athletes who left your program to understand their reasons
- Assess your current crisis prevention and response systems

Document your findings and identify the three most critical areas where your program needs systematic attention before problems escalate.

Chapter 2

Defining Civility in Sports—What Character Looks Like Under Pressure

The Day Civility Meant Survival

Years after Victor was stabbed, I watched an eight-year-old stagger off a summer tournament field in Atlanta, his face flushed red, sweat gone—classic heat exhaustion. His father grabbed his shoulders: "Don't be weak. Get back out there." The coach didn't intervene. Other parents shouted about pickle juice and toughing it out.

I ran down from the press box. "He needs immediate cooling. Now."

"This is my son," the father said, grip tightening.

"And this is what heat stroke looks like right before it kills children."

The boy's eyes found mine—wide, trusting, desperate. Eight years old and already learning his worth was measured by his willingness to endure what adults demanded.

No medical personnel. No heat protocol. No plan. Just hundreds of students competing in dangerous conditions while adults prioritized entertainment over safety.

That moment crystallized something: civility isn't about being nice. It's about choosing humanity when everything around you is falling apart.

Real Strength Doesn't Yell

Most people think civility makes programs soft because they've never seen what real strength looks like under pressure. They confuse aggression with intensity, intimidation with motivation, and cruelty with toughness.

Civility in sports is the conscious discipline of modeling respect, accountability, and character under pressure at every level of a sports organization. It's the ability to compete with maximum intensity while remembering that opponents are human beings, not obstacles. It means coaching with passion while treating athletes with dignity. It means wanting to win without being willing to destroy people to get there.

Real toughness is helping an opponent up after a hard foul. Real intensity is maintaining focus during poor officiating instead of losing control. Real strength is encouraging teammates through mistakes instead of tearing them down.

The most competitive athletes I've known were also the most civil because they understood that peak performance requires calm minds, not chaotic emotions.

We Cheered for the Wrong Things

But if this definition is so clear, why does confusion persist? Because our entire sports culture has been built on a false foundation.

Our sports culture has systematically confused intensity with aggression for so long that many people can't imagine competitive excellence without emotional abuse. We've watched too many coaches throw tantrums on television and called it passion. We've seen too many parents scream at referees and labeled it caring. We've observed too many athletes trash-talk opponents and termed it confidence.

But research consistently shows that these behaviors actually impair performance. Studies analyzing track and field athletes during the European Games found that increased cortisol levels prior to competition were detrimental to athletic performance[13]. Athletes operating under chronic stress show 23% slower reaction times and 31% decreased decision-making accuracy compared to those competing from positive emotional states[14].

The "tough love" approach doesn't create mental toughness—it creates mental interference that prevents athletes from accessing their full potential when they need it most.

"I Turned Out Fine" and Other Lies

Some coaches will read this and think I'm soft. They'll point to legendary programs built on discipline, demanding standards, and tough love. "My coach screamed at me, and I turned out fine," they'll say. "Kids today are too sensitive."

Here's what they miss: demanding excellence isn't

the same as degrading people. There's a difference between high standards and humiliation, between accountability and abuse, between intensity and intimidation.

The coaches they remember as "tough but effective" usually had something else too: they cared visibly, showed up consistently, and never made athletes question their fundamental worth. The screaming wasn't what worked. The relationship was.

And here's the uncomfortable truth: many people who say they "turned out fine" didn't. They developed anxiety around performance. They struggle with self-worth tied to achievement. They parent or coach the same way because unexamined trauma becomes inherited tradition.

Real toughness isn't making athletes afraid of you. It's teaching them they're capable of more than they believed possible—and standing with them while they discover it.

1936: Civility in the Face of Fascism

These aren't just numbers on a page. History shows us what's possible when athletes choose a different path—even under the most extreme pressure.

The most influential examples of sports civility emerged during periods of intense social tension, when individual athletes chose to transcend the prejudices and pressures of their era.

At the 1936 Berlin Olympics, American sprinter Jesse Owens and German long jumper Carl "Luz" Long formed a friendship that defied Nazi racial ideology. After Owens fouled twice in qualifying, facing elimination, Long advised him to move his takeoff mark back several inches to avoid another foul. Long's counsel helped Owens set an Olympic record and win gold, with Long taking silver and becoming the first to congratulate his competitor[15].

Their friendship continued through letters until Long's death in 1943 during World War II. Owens later said he would "melt down all the medals and cups" he had for "the twenty-four-carat friendship" he felt for Long.

That's civility under the ultimate pressure: competing to win while refusing to see your opponent as your enemy.

On the Field, In the Fire

That 1936 example might feel distant, but civility under pressure looks the same today—just in different uniforms, on different fields.

Here's what civility looks like in real athletic situations:

During close competition, civil athletes maintain focus on execution rather than external factors. They support teammates through mistakes rather than showing frustration. They acknowledge good plays by opponents even while competing fiercely.

With controversial officiating, civil programs accept calls with dignity while continuing to compete at maximum intensity. They address officials respectfully when seeking clarification. They maintain focus on controllable factors rather than dwelling on calls they can't change.

After defeats, civil competitors congratulate opponents genuinely for their success. They take responsibility for preparation and execution. They use losses as learning experiences that build resilience rather than bitter experiences that create resentment.

During team conflicts, civil programs address issues directly but respectfully. They focus on behaviors and impacts rather than character attacks. They seek solutions that honor everyone's dignity while strengthening team chemistry.

Winning More by Screaming Less

Research consistently shows that civil athletic programs achieve better competitive results over time. When athletes feel psychologically safe, they take appropriate risks that lead to breakthrough performances. When coaches model respect under pressure, athletes learn emotional regulation skills that help them perform better in crucial moments. When parents support rather than pressure, young athletes develop intrinsic motivation that sustains them through challenges.

Teams with positive cultures also tend to have

better chemistry, which translates directly to competitive advantage. Research analyzing over 15,000 coaching behaviors found that positive reinforcement and supportive coaching dimensions significantly predict athlete satisfaction and development outcomes[16].

How to Teach the Hardest Thing

Civility under pressure requires specific skills that can be practiced and improved:

Emotional regulation training includes breathing techniques that activate the parasympathetic nervous system, self-talk strategies that maintain perspective during challenging moments, and mental rehearsal of appropriate responses to likely pressure situations.

Communication under pressure involves tone management that maintains respect even when expressing disagreement, active listening that hears others' perspectives completely before responding, and de-escalation techniques that reduce rather than escalate conflict.

Perspective-taking skills enable understanding of opponents' situations, recognition of officials' difficult jobs, awareness of teammates' different stress responses, and appreciation for parents' deep caring even when it's expressed inappropriately.

When Character Cracks

I learned these principles the hard way—by watching what happened when we abandoned them entirely.

What the Gym Fell Silent For

I can pinpoint the exact moment I realized we had confused brutality for strength.

It was during the fourth quarter of a regional championship game. Our point guard, Jasmine, had just thrown her third turnover in five minutes. The game was slipping away, scholarship dreams evaporating with each mistake.

Coach Reynolds cupped his hands around his mouth and shouted across the gymnasium, his voice cutting through the crowd noise like a blade: "Jasmine! My dead grandmother could run this offense better than you!"

The gymnasium fell silent. Not the good kind of silence—the terrible kind that settles over a room when everyone realizes they've witnessed something that can't be taken back.

Jasmine's shoulders sagged. The fight went out of her eyes. She played the remaining minutes like someone waiting for permission to disappear.

We lost by twelve points. But we lost something more important: the trust of a seventeen-year-old who had given everything to a sport that devoured her dignity in return.

After the game, I found Reynolds in the hallway. "That was cruel," I said.

"That was coaching," he replied. "Sometimes you have to break them down to build them back up."

But Jasmine never came back up. She quit basketball two weeks later, despite being recruited by three Division I schools. Years later, she expressed that she still heard Reynolds' voice whenever she faced pressure situations in her professional life—not as motivation, but as a reminder that her worth was always one mistake away from destruction.

Civility isn't about being nice. It's about refusing to destroy people in pursuit of goals that don't ultimately matter more than the people pursuing them.

We Mistook Rage for Leadership

We trace the moment competition became contaminated—when did healthy intensity curdle into destructive rage?

Somewhere along the way, we started celebrating the coach throwing chairs instead of the one building confidence. We began admiring the parent who "fought for their kid" by screaming at referees instead of the one who modeled G.R.A.C.E under pressure. We confused volume with conviction, hostility with heart.

Civility is a muscle we let atrophy in favor of rage. We practiced anger until it became our default response to disappointment. We rehearsed blame until it became more natural than accountability. We perfected the art of making other people responsible for our feelings.

But muscles can be rebuilt.

Love, Weaponized by Fear

Her name was Jennifer, and she cornered me in the school parking lot after her son's team lost their homecoming game.

"This is bullshit, Alva." Her voice shook with the kind of rage that comes from love twisted into expectation. "Tyler worked his ass off all summer. He deserves better than eight minutes of garbage time."

I could see Tyler in my peripheral vision, forty feet away by their SUV, shoulders hunched with the particular shame of teenage boys whose parents have become their biggest embarrassment.

"Jennifer," I said quietly, "Tyler can hear us."

"Good. Maybe he needs to hear someone fighting for him since his coach won't."

"He needs to see someone who loves him regardless of playing time. He needs to learn that his worth isn't measured in minutes on a clock."

Jennifer's face crumpled. "I just... I want him to succeed. I want colleges to notice him."

"They will. But not if you teach him that love is conditional on performance."

We stood there in the parking lot under the fluorescent lights, two adults who cared deeply about a seventeen-year-old boy, trying to figure out how caring had become so complicated. How protection had transformed into pressure. How love had learned to wear the mask of demand.

Tyler got a full scholarship to a Division II school the following year. Not because his mother fought harder, but because he learned to compete without the weight of her desperation on his shoulders.

Chapter 3

From Wreckage to G.R.A.C.E

Through years of working, reading, and researching strategies and theories to address the root causes, not just the symptoms of what we were facing, patterns began to emerge. Little by little, as I tried weaving different pieces of character work into our daily grind, I started to recognize the rhythm of what truly stuck and what fell flat. Programs that successfully integrated competitive excellence with character development shared certain characteristics, which I eventually organized into what became the G.R.A.C.E framework.

This wasn't an academic exercise or theoretical model—it emerged from practical necessity. The night Victor was stabbed, I sat in a hospital waiting room wondering what could have stopped it. Security? Maybe. Metal detectors? Possibly. But deeper than policies and protocols, there was a **cultural failure**. A slow rot we'd accepted. Pressure without preparation. Performance without support. Toughness without care.

And in that waiting room, one word kept repeating itself in my head: **G.R.A.C.E.**

I kept thinking about G.R.A.C.E and mercy—that unmerited favor, those second chances—which was needed for him to survive and have a full recovery.

That's what Victor deserved. That's what his attacker should have received years earlier.

What emerged over time wasn't a slogan, or an acronym for the sake of branding. G.R.A.C.E isn't just a word. Its a framework, built from the ground up, inside locker rooms, team meetings, conflict resolutions, and one painfully learned lesson after another. G.R.A.C.E means unmerited favor—giving people what they need to succeed rather than what we think they deserve based on performance alone. It means creating space for human beings to fail, learn, grow, and transform without being destroyed in the process.

In athletics, this translates to creating environments where athletes are valued as human beings first, competitors second. Where coaches model the character they seek to develop. Where parents support rather than pressure. Where competition becomes a laboratory for character development rather than a crucible that burns people up.

The G.R.A.C.E framework rests on the understanding that competitive excellence and human dignity aren't opposites—they're partners. G.R.A.C.E doesn't mean lowering standards. It means raising people up to meet them. It means believing that athletes can be held accountable without being shamed, that mistakes can be corrected without destroying confidence, that intensity can coexist with integrity.

G.R.A.C.E means recognizing that the young person standing in front of you—sweaty, exhausted, devastated by a loss—is somebody's entire world. That how you respond in this moment will echo in their life long after the final score is forgotten. That your words have the power to build or destroy, and you get to choose which legacy you leave.

The five principles of G.R.A.C.E work together to create cultures where excellence and character thrive:

What G.R.A.C.E Is (and Is Not)

G.R.A.C.E isn't softness.

G.R.A.C.E is not about lowering the bar.
It's about **raising people up to meet it**—with dignity intact.

It's not leniency.
It's **structure with compassion**.

And it's not about letting things slide.
It's about **correcting without destroying**.

G.R.A.C.E is how we build athletes who are:

- Fierce and respectful
- Accountable and unashamed
- Competitive and grounded
- Leaders in sport and life

Each letter is a principle. Together, they're a culture.

G – Goodwill: Assume Effort Before Blame

Most kids aren't trying to fail.
 Most parents aren't trying to sabotage.
 Most officials aren't trying to get it wrong.

Goodwill is the decision to begin with belief, not suspicion.

When a player makes a mistake, assume they're learning—not lazy.
 When a parent is upset, assume they care—even if they misfire.
 When an opponent celebrates, assume they're proud—not mocking.

> Psychological safety isn't softness.
> It's what makes risk—and growth—possible.

We correct. We coach. But we start with belief.

R – Respect: Dignity Is Not Conditional

Respect is not earned.
 Not on the bench. Not from parents. Not from officials.

Respect is the floor. Not the reward.

- Speak to athletes like you'd want someone to speak to your child.
- Honor the opponent who makes competition possible.
- Treat every person in the gym like their presence matters.

From the team captain to the timekeeper, **dignity is non-negotiable**.

A – Accountability: Correct Without Shaming

Accountability isn't about punishment.
It's about **ownership**—of choices, outcomes, and impact.

But here's the rule:
Accountability without shame.

Because shame is identity-based: *"You are the mistake."*
Accountability is behavioral: *"That mistake can be fixed."*

We teach athletes:

- Own it

- Learn from it

- Adjust

- Move on

This is where resilience is built—not in tearing down, but in telling the truth *without cutting into self-worth*.

C – Civility: Hold Your Character Under Pressure

Anyone can behave when they're up by 20.

Civility is how you act when the game is tied, the call is bad, and your ego wants revenge.

This is the hardest principle in the framework—and the most visible.

- Coaches: Can you hold your tone when the ref blows it?

- Athletes: Can you stay present when frustration boils?

- Parents: Can you support without inserting shame?

Civility is discipline—not decorum.
It's the habit of staying human in moments that invite something worse.

E – Excellence: Push for More Without Pushing People Away

Excellence isn't just about winning.

It's about helping people become the best version of themselves—on and off the field.

- Excellence means challenging with care.

- Excellence means praising growth, not just results.

- Excellence means pushing performance *and* character, not one at the expense of the other.

You can win the game and lose the team.
Or you can build a program that wins *and lasts.*

Because when athletes feel safe, seen, and challenged—they'll give you everything they've got.

And more importantly, they'll carry it forward into every area of their lives.

The Scar That Spoke

Several years later, Victor Thompson returned to his alma mater with an education degree and a vision that transformed trauma into purpose. I watched him lead his first parent meeting as an assistant coach, his scars visible on his forearms but his voice steady with conviction.

"I want to tell you why I'm here," he said to the group gathered in the gymnasium. "Five or more years ago, someone tried to take my life right outside this building. But this place also saved it. The coaches who visited me in the hospital. The teammates who never let me quit on myself. The principal who showed me that one terrible night doesn't define what a school can become."

The gymnasium was silent. Parents who had come to complain about playing time or to question coaching decisions found themselves face-to-face with the living consequence of unchecked cultural toxicity.

"Your children will face moments that test their character," Victor continued. "How we respond to those moments as parents, as coaches, as a community that's what shapes them. Not the score on any scoreboard."

In the audience, I saw parents wiping their eyes. Coaches nodding with understanding. Board members finally comprehending that youth athletics isn't about games, it's about the people we're raising to inherit our world.

This is where hope lives: in the space between trauma and transformation, in the choice to build something better from the wreckage of what failed.

The Culture You Choose, Every Day

I've learned that civility isn't something you can demand—it's something you must model, teach, and practice until it becomes automatic. The programs that successfully develop civil competitors are those that understand it's a skill set requiring as much attention and development as any physical technique.

The key insight is that civility enhances rather than inhibits competitive performance. When athletes learn to channel competitive fire constructively, when they develop emotional regulation skills, when they practice maintaining character under pressure, they become more effective competitors, not less.

The choice is ours. Every day, in every interaction, we decide what kind of culture we're building. We choose whether to pass on trauma or transformation. We determine whether the next generation learns that winning requires destroying others or that true excellence emerges when we lift each other up.

G.R.A.C.E isn't weakness. It's the hardest work there is—choosing humanity when everything around you says otherwise.

Reflection Questions

1. **Personal Definition:** How do you currently define civility in your specific sport context? Is your definition focused on surface behaviors or deeper character development?

2. **Pressure Point Analysis:** Think about your last challenging competition. How did you and your athletes respond when things went wrong? Did your behavior reflect the civility you claim to value?

3. **Culture vs. Competition:** Do you believe civility makes athletes less competitive, or can intense competition and civil behavior coexist? What evidence supports your belief?

4. **Historical Inspiration:** Which examples of civility under pressure most inspire you? How could you use these stories to teach athletes about competing with character?

Chapter Assignment

Civility Assessment Exercise: For one week, document specific examples of civil and uncivil behavior you observe in your program and broader athletic community. Include:

- How coaches respond to athlete mistakes during pressure situations

- How athletes treat opponents, officials, and teammates during challenging moments
- How parents and spectators behave when games aren't going their way
- How your program handles conflicts or controversial situations

Analyze your observations: What patterns do you notice? Where are the biggest opportunities for improvement? What would need to change for civility to become more natural and automatic in your program culture?

Chapter 4

Parental Responsibility in Creating Civil Sports Culture

When Shame Sounds Like Love

During my second year of developing what would become the G.R.A.C.E framework, I watched a father completely lose control during his son's basketball game. The student was having a rough night—missed shots, turnovers, defensive lapses. With five minutes left and his team down by twelve, the father leaned over the railing and screamed:

"You're embarrassing yourself! Your 6 year old sister could play better than this!"

I walked over during a timeout. "Mr. Williams, step outside with me."

"I'm just trying to motivate my son."

"No, you're humiliating him. And you're teaching him that your love depends on his performance."

The man's face changed. "I... I didn't think about it that way."

"Your son is going to remember this game for years. Not the score, not the stats—how his father treated him when things went wrong. What do you want him to remember?"

His son finished the game poorly from a statistical standpoint. But he kept trying, kept communicating, kept his head up. After the final buzzer, his father was the first person to tell him he was proud.

We lost by twelve. But we won something more important.

Where the Real Game Gets Lost

The most visible breakdown of civility in youth sports often occurs not on the field, but in the stands. Research from the National Association of Sports Officials reveals that 40% of officials cite parent behavior as the primary reason for leaving their positions[17], creating an official shortage that threatens the foundation of youth athletics.

But the impact goes far beyond official retention. Athletes frequently report feeling embarrassed by inappropriate parent conduct. Coaches spend significant time managing parent conflicts rather than teaching skills. Officials avoid certain programs due to hostile spectator environments. Younger siblings often refuse to participate after witnessing negative parent behavior.

Most concerning, research consistently shows that parental behavior during competition directly affects young athletes' stress responses and performance. When children perceive criticism or disappointment from parents, elevated cortisol and stress hormone responses can impair decision-making capacity, physical coordination, ability to learn from mistakes, and team communication[18].

When Parenting Becomes a Business Plan

Youth sports have become a massive financial

investment for families. Travel teams can cost thousands of dollars annually. Private coaching, showcases, equipment, the expenses add up quickly, creating what I call the "return on investment mentality."

When families have invested that much money, every missed shot feels like wasted dollars. Every benching feels like theft. Every loss feels like a bad return on investment.

"We paid twelve thousand dollars for this season," one mother screamed at me when her daughter was benched for unsportsmanlike conduct. "She better play every minute, or I want my money back!"

The pay-to-play mentality has turned children into commodities and parents into investors expecting returns measured in playing time and college scholarships that statistically won't materialize. Only about 2% of high school athletes receive college athletic scholarships, and less than 1% of college athletes make it to professional sports[19].

What the Data Proves—and Kids Already Know

Dr. John Gottman's relationship research reveals that positive interactions must outnumber negative ones by at least 5:1 for healthy dynamics[20]. This ratio applies directly to parent-child athletic relationships, but many parents operate from exactly the opposite approach—offering one encouragement for every five criticisms.

Studies show that children unconsciously mirror adult emotional regulation patterns. In athletic settings, negative parental modeling often creates athletes who:

- Blame officials for poor outcomes
- Show increased on-field arguing and unsportsmanlike conduct
- Demonstrate resistance to coaching feedback
- Have higher dropout rates in youth sports

Conversely, positive parental modeling tends to develop athletes who:

- Accept responsibility for performance
- Interact respectfully with opponents and officials
- Demonstrate openness to learning and improvement
- Sustain participation through challenges

The Parenting Timeout

1. Master the 24-Hour Rule

Don't talk about the game immediately afterward. Emotions are running high for everyone, you, your child, coaches, and teammates. Nothing good comes from immediate analysis. Wait a day. Let everyone process what happened. Then focus on effort and character, not outcomes.

Research indicates that immediate post-game conversations often occur when emotions are heightened, leading to increased conflict and reduced learning. Waiting allows for perspective and reduces the likelihood of saying something you'll regret.

2. Change Your Language

The words you use teach lessons about what matters most:

- **Stop saying:** "You should have made that shot." **Start saying:** "I loved watching you compete."
- **Stop saying:** "The referee cost you the game." **Start saying:** "You handled that disappointment well."
- **Stop saying:** "You weren't trying hard enough." **Start saying:** "What did you learn about yourself today?"

3. Model What You Want to See

Students watch how parents handle stress, disappointment, and conflict. They're learning more from behavior in the stands than from any lecture they'll receive in the car. Every reaction becomes a teaching moment about character, resilience, and what it means to be part of a community.

Building the Stands That Hold the Team

Through working with hundreds of families, I've identified five essential areas where parents can make the difference between toxic and transformative athletic experiences:

Pillar 1: Emotional Regulation and Self-Awareness

The key is developing awareness of your triggers and having strategies for managing intense emotions. Before each event, set specific intentions for your behavior. Practice deep breathing techniques you can use during tense moments. Remember that your child's worth isn't determined by athletic performance.

Pillar 2: Understanding Role Boundaries

Your role as a parent spectator is to:

- Provide unconditional emotional support regardless of performance
- Celebrate effort and character demonstration
- Model appropriate behavior for other spectators
- Support coaches and officials publicly while addressing concerns privately through proper channels

What's NOT your role:

- Coaching from the sidelines during games
- Questioning officials' decisions publicly
- Comparing your child's performance to teammates
- Negotiating playing time during competitions

Pillar 3: Positive Communication and Support Systems

Use growth-focused language that celebrates process over outcome. Instead of "I can't believe you missed that opportunity," try "I noticed how you encouraged your teammate when they made a mistake." Focus on effort, improvement, and character development rather than statistics and winning.

Pillar 4: Cultural Leadership and Influence

Take ownership of your section and gently redirect other parents when they cross behavioral lines. Model positive responses to officiating calls, opponent success, and team struggles. Create informal networks of parents committed to supporting positive culture rather than contributing to toxic environments.

Pillar 5: Long-Term Perspective and Character Development

Help your child identify transferable skills from athletics: teamwork, perseverance, handling disappointment, leadership development. Connect athletic experiences to broader character development and life preparation. Celebrate moments when your child shows integrity, even if it costs the team competitively.

They're Always Watching

Research from multiple studies on social learning demonstrates that children unconsciously mirror adult emotional regulation patterns[21]. What you do speaks so much louder than what you say that your children can't hear what you're saying.

If you want athletes who accept responsibility, you must model accountability when things go wrong. If you want competitors who respect officials, you must demonstrate that respect consistently. If you want teammates who support each other through mistakes, you must show G.R.A.C.E when your own child struggles.

Beyond the Buzzer

Most parents say they want sports to teach their children life skills, but then they focus exclusively on short-term outcomes. The lessons that matter: resilience, teamwork, handling adversity, only come when character development takes priority over immediate results.

Twenty years from now, your child won't remember most of the games they played. But they'll remember how you treated them when they made mistakes. They'll carry forward the lessons you taught them about handling disappointment, supporting teammates, and maintaining dignity under pressure.

When Love Looks Like Pressure

Parents who struggle most with appropriate sideline

behavior are often those who care most deeply about their children. Their love gets expressed as pressure because they want so badly for their kids to succeed. The key is helping them understand that support serves success better than pressure, and that character development is success.

The most effective parent education happens through example rather than instruction. When other parents see positive sideline behavior leading to better athlete performance and family relationships, they become more open to examining their own approaches.

Reflection Questions

1. **Emotional Regulation Assessment:** What specific situations during games or practices trigger your strongest emotional responses? What strategies could help you maintain composure during these moments?

2. **Role Boundary Evaluation:** Do you ever find yourself coaching from the sidelines, questioning officials publicly, or overstepping appropriate parent boundaries? What would help you stay within supportive roles?

3. **Communication Pattern Analysis:** When you talk with your child about athletics, what ratio of positive to critical comments do you typically use? How could you increase

positive, growth-focused language?

4. **Long-Term Perspective Check:** What do you want your child to remember about their athletic experience in 20 years? How does your current approach align with creating those memories?

Chapter Assignment

Parent Behavior Audit: For two weeks, keep a written record of your interactions related to your child's athletic participation:

- Document what you say to your child before, during, and after competitions
- Note your emotional responses to officiating, coaching decisions, and your child's performance
- Record examples of your sideline behavior and communication with other parents
- Track your child's responses to different types of support you provide

Analyze your patterns: Where do you see opportunities to better support your child's development? What changes would most improve your family's athletic experience? How can you become a more positive influence on your program's culture?

Chapter 5

When Everyone Shares Responsibility - The Broader Ecosystem

When the Internet Comes for Your Kids

One year into developing the systematic culture approach that would become the G.R.A.C.E framework, I thought my programs had figured out a positive culture. Then screenshots of threatening messages targeting my student-athletes went viral on social media. Within hours, the posts had been shared thousands of times, with comment threads full of harassment that went far beyond sports.

That's when I realized that creating positive culture inside programs wasn't enough. I was fighting battles on multiple fronts, and I needed allies I hadn't even considered.

The online harassment began after a controversial call during a playoff game. One parent started posting about "incompetent officials" and "kids who don't deserve to win." Others amplified the message, adding increasingly toxic commentary. Soon, my athletes were receiving direct threats and personal attacks from people they'd never met.

Within 48 hours, the story had morphed completely. What started as frustration about officiating became a character assassination of teenage athletes who had given everything for their teams. Anonymous accounts were posting personal information about players, creating harassment campaigns that followed them into school and their part-time jobs.

I couldn't address this through internal culture work alone. I needed:

- Social media platforms to enforce community standards
- Governing bodies to address the harassment at its source
- My community to counter negativity with support
- Better security protocols for subsequent events

That crisis taught me that sustainable culture change requires coordination across multiple systems, not just hoping individual programs can overcome toxic environments they didn't create.

Who's Actually in the Arena

1. Clicks Over Character

These companies profit from engagement, and conflict generates more clicks than character. Research suggests that negative content often spreads faster than positive content online[22]. The platforms have the technology to address harassment in real-time, they choose not to use it consistently.

When my athletes faced online harassment, I learned that:

- Reporting systems are often inadequate
- Responses are slow and inconsistent
- The damage spreads faster than any intervention can contain it

- Platforms that allow sports content need sports-specific community standards and enforcement protocols

2. Rules Without Teeth

State athletic associations and league commissioners set the rules, but most don't enforce them consistently. They issue strong statements about sportsmanship while allowing the same programs to violate standards repeatedly without meaningful consequences.

I've seen leagues where certain coaches are known for poor behavior, but they keep coaching because they win games. I've watched organizations implement zero-tolerance policies that are selectively enforced based on politics rather than principles. When governing bodies fail to maintain standards, individual programs can't create culture islands that survive in toxic ecosystems.

3. The Crowd Teaches Too

Every reaction teaches young athletes something about what matters to their community. When adults model appropriate responses to adversity, students learn resilience. When they model tantrums, students learn that disappointment justifies bad behavior.

The community that rallied around my athletes during the social media crisis showed me the power of collective action. Parents, teachers, local business owners, and even opposing teams' families stepped up to counter the negativity with support. That response taught our athletes more about community values than any team meeting could have accomplished.

4. The Architecture of Behavior

Physical design affects behavior more than most people realize. Facilities where spectators sit directly behind players' benches experience 67% more coach-fan incidents than those with buffer zones. Poor sight lines create more disputes. Crowded concession areas generate conflicts during peak times.

But thoughtful design creates opposite effects:

- Family sections reduce exposure to inappropriate language
- Buffer zones on baselines, endzones and sidelines reduce direct physical and verbal interactions between fans and players
- Dedicated parking for officials prevents confrontations before and after games
- Enhanced lighting in parking areas increases security and reduces post-game incidents

What Real Partnership Requires

Real culture change requires all these groups working together, not separately. When my athletes faced the harassment campaign, effective response required:

- **Platform accountability:** Real-time monitoring and response to harassment during live events
- **Governing body support:** Clear policies about harassment that follows athletes beyond the playing field
- **Community engagement:** Positive voices that outnumber and overwhelm negative ones
- **Facility partnerships:** Enhanced security and communication protocols for subsequent events

The most successful culture transformations involves athletic directors who understood they needed to build coalitions rather than trying to change culture in isolation.

No More Culture Islands

The four external forces don't operate independently. Social media amplifies what happens at facilities. Governing bodies set standards that fans either support or undermine. Facilities create environments where digital behavior gets reinforced or discouraged.

Success requires coordination across all stakeholders, with shared accountability frameworks that connect efforts rather than duplicate them.

Communication Protocols: Establish real-time communication systems between all stakeholders during events. When facility staff identify problems, social media monitors can track digital spread. When governing bodies issue penalties, fan groups can reinforce appropriate community standards.

Incident Documentation: Create standardized reporting that feeds back to all stakeholders for continuous improvement. Every incident becomes a learning opportunity for prevention rather than just punishment for violation.

Community Engagement: Regular forums where all stakeholders address issues, share solutions, and commit to collective action. Make sports culture improvement a community-wide responsibility rather than a burden for individual programs.

Outcome Measurement: Quarterly assessments of program effectiveness with public transparency. Track progress across all four external forces and adjust strategies based on evidence rather than assumptions.

Winning Together, or Losing Alone

Social Media Engagement Strategy

Rather than waiting for platforms to police themselves, proactive programs create positive content strategies that crowd out negativity. This includes:

- Celebrating character alongside performance

- Sharing stories of athletes overcoming challenges through perseverance rather than talent alone
- Highlighting examples of positive sportsmanship and community support
- Creating hashtags and campaigns that emphasize growth and development

Governing Body Collaboration

Effective athletic directors don't just follow policies, they help shape them. This involves:

- Participating in governance committees and rule-making processes
- Providing feedback about policy effectiveness and enforcement gaps
- Sharing successful culture development strategies with other programs
- Advocating for resources and training that support positive culture development

Community Culture Building

Programs that successfully develop external support focus on education rather than just enforcement. They:

- Provide parent education programs that teach positive support techniques
- Create recognition systems for positive fan behavior and community contributions

- Partner with local organizations that share similar values and character development goals
- Host community events that showcase athlete character alongside competitive achievement

Facility Partnership Development

Rather than just renting space, culture-focused programs work with facilities to create environments that support their values. This includes:

- Advocating for design changes that promote positive interactions
- Providing security training that emphasizes de-escalation rather than confrontation
- Creating signage and environmental cues that reinforce respect and sportsmanship
- Establishing protocols for addressing problems before they escalate to require law enforcement

When the Right Culture Goes Viral

When these partnerships work effectively, the impact extends far beyond individual athletic programs:

- Communities develop reputations for positive sports culture that attract families seeking healthy environments for their children
- Officials request assignments at venues known for respectful treatment

- Businesses want to sponsor programs that represent values they want to support

Most importantly, young people learn that entire communities can work together to create something positive, demonstrating lessons about civic engagement and collective responsibility that extend far beyond athletics.

Start Small, Prove the Point

Building these external partnerships requires patience and persistence. Many stakeholders are dealing with their own challenges and may not initially understand how they can contribute to positive sports culture. The key is helping them see the connections between their interests and your program's success.

The most effective approach is starting small with willing partners and letting success create momentum for broader engagement. When people see concrete benefits from coordination, they become advocates for expanding the approach to other areas and programs.

Reflection Questions

1. **Partnership Assessment:** Which of these four external groups currently supports positive culture in your community, and which ones undermine it? What specific evidence supports your assessment?

2. **Coordination Opportunities:** What partnerships could you develop that would strengthen each group's support for civil sports culture? What would you need to offer to make these partnerships mutually beneficial?

3. **Crisis Response:** How would you coordinate response if your program faced a crisis involving multiple stakeholder groups? What communication systems would you need, and who would need to be involved?

4. **Community Impact:** What would it look like if all four external groups actively supported your program values? How would that change the experience for athletes, families, and coaches?

Chapter Assignment

Ecosystem Mapping Exercise: Create a comprehensive map of all stakeholders who influence culture in your athletic program:

- Identify specific individuals and organizations in each of the four categories
- Assess their current impact on your program culture (positive, negative, or neutral)
- Research their interests, challenges, and priorities to understand potential partnership opportunities

- Develop specific outreach strategies for building relationships with key stakeholders
- Create an action plan for coordinating efforts across all four groups

Present your findings to program leadership and begin implementation of the highest-priority partnership opportunities.

Chapter 6

The Business Case for Civility – Culture as Competitive Advantage.

The Silent Budget Bleed

Most athletic organizations track obvious expenses — salaries, insurance, equipment. But they rarely account for the **hidden costs of toxic culture**, like:

- **Coach Turnover**: High turnover means recruitment costs, training gaps, and program instability.

- **Legal Risk**: Even minor harassment claims cost thousands in defense. The major cases can be catastrophic.

- **Referee Shortages**: Poor sportsmanship raises officiating costs — or leaves games uncovered.

- **Brand Damage**: One viral video of sideline chaos can undo years of community trust.

- **Athlete Dropout**: When 70% of kids quit sports by age 13, that's not just sad — it's a pipeline collapse.

Programs don't collapse because of a single bad season. They bleed slowly, invisibly, until they're empty.

The Math of Doing the Right Thing

Programs that prioritize **systematic culture**

development don't just survive — they grow.

- **Retention gains**: A 25% improvement in athlete retention can mean $50,000+ in recovered revenue for mid-sized programs.

- **Referral growth**: Strong cultures create satisfied families who recruit others. Many programs grow 15% annually this way — without spending a dime on marketing.

- **Premium pricing**: Parents will pay more for environments where their child is treated like a human, not a stat line.

- **Crisis savings**: Fewer emergencies, fewer interventions, less money spent on damage control.

The real business case for civility? It **costs less to do things right**.

Not Just a Pizza Party and Trust Falls

Let's be clear: culture change isn't about "team bonding" or motivational posters.

It's about **trainable, repeatable skills**:

- **Communication under pressure**: Giving feedback that builds instead of breaks.

- **Conflict resolution**: Addressing root causes, not symptoms.

- **Emotional regulation**: Modeling the behavior you want under stress.

- **Cultural competence**: Creating inclusive environments that welcome, not marginalize.

These aren't soft skills. They're **performance multipliers** — and they're coachable.

Brains on the Bench

Neuroscience backs this up: chronic stress **diminishes performance**. Under stress, reaction times slow by 23%, decision-making drops by 31%, and the brain literally shifts away from problem-solving.

On the other hand, positive coaching environments light up the parts of the brain responsible for **focus, memory, and motor coordination**. The science is clear: athletes play better when they feel safe, seen, and supported.

How Character Wins Games

Let's stop pretending character and competition are enemies.

- **Team Chemistry**: Trust leads to communication. Support leads to accountability. Healthy teams beat talented ones all the time.

- **Individual Performance**: Athletes with emotional regulation perform better under pressure. Athletes who trust their coaches **learn faster.**

- **Recruitment Power**: Families want more than trophies — they want mentors. Culture-forward programs attract better athletes and better parents.

Winning isn't the cost of character. It's often the result of it.

The Compound Interest of Culture

The impact of culture compounds over time:

- **Alumni return as donors and coaches.**
- **Communities invest in programs that reflect their values.**
- **Staff stay longer when they aren't emotionally exhausted.**
- **Crises get prevented, not managed.**

A single investment in culture has ripple effects that last for decades.

What Success *Actually* Looks Like

Want to measure return on civility? Track this:

Financial Metrics

- Retention and referral revenue
- Reduced legal and crisis costs
- Fundraising growth
- Premium pricing capacity

Performance Metrics

- Team success rooted in positive practices
- Coach growth and retention
- Athlete improvement and long-term participation

Culture Metrics

- Conflict rates
- Feedback from officials and parents
- Alumni satisfaction

- Athlete well-being post-participation

When culture and performance are measured together, success becomes sustainable.

The Story That Changes the Board's Mind

Sometimes, the spreadsheet isn't enough. The case that convinces a board or a business owner isn't a line item — it's a life changed.

It's the athlete who came back to coach because his coach believed in him.
The parent who stopped screaming and started supporting.
The team that lost the championship but gained their dignity.

When you show that character creates competitive advantage — on the field, in the books, and in the lives of young people — people stop asking, "Is it worth it?"

They start asking, "Why didn't we do this sooner?"

Reflection Questions

1. **Hidden Cost Assessment:** What has toxic culture actually cost your program in terms of lost participation, coach turnover, community relations, and crisis management? Can you quantify these

expenses?

2. **Investment vs. Expense:** How much do you currently spend dealing with problems versus preventing them? What would change if you invested proactively in culture development?

3. **ROI Projection:** If you achieved similar results to documented successful programs (improved retention, reduced conflicts, enhanced reputation), what would be your projected financial benefit over three years?

4. **Competitive Advantage Analysis:** What advantages would your program gain by being known for both competitive excellence and character development? How would that affect recruitment, community support, and long-term sustainability?

Chapter Assignment

Culture Cost-Benefit Analysis: Conduct a comprehensive financial assessment of culture impact on your program:

Cost Analysis:

- Calculate actual expenses from coach turnover, behavioral incidents, and reputation management in the past three years

- Estimate lost revenue from participant dropout and negative word-of-mouth
- Assess premium costs for officials, security, and crisis management due to culture problems

Benefit Projection:

- Research successful programs with strong cultures to benchmark potential improvements
- Calculate potential revenue increases from better retention and referral growth
- Estimate cost savings from reduced conflicts, crises, and staff turnover
- Project long-term benefits from enhanced community support and premium positioning

Implementation Planning:

- Develop budget for systematic culture development initiatives
- Create timeline for implementation and measurement of results
- Identify funding sources and stakeholder investment opportunities
- Establish metrics for tracking return on culture investment

Present your analysis to program leadership with specific recommendations for culture development investment and expected returns.

Chapter 7

Character Under Fire—When Values Meet Reality

CHARACTER UNDER FIRE: Peace Over Pride

Two years after implementing systematic culture change, I got a 2 AM call from Metro Police. Three of my basketball players had been involved in a fight at a restaurant—but not how I expected.

Players from two rival schools had started going at it over trash talk from an earlier game. Instead of joining in or walking away, my students stepped between them and talked them down.

"These young men potentially prevented serious injuries," Officer Johnson told me. "They showed remarkable maturity and leadership. They used conflict resolution techniques. I wish more adults practiced."

This was character under fire—teenagers who'd learned that real strength means protecting others, not dominating them. Young people who understood that their values would be tested in precisely these moments when emotions run high and easy choices feel justified.

The incident became a defining moment for our program. Not because my players avoided trouble, but because they actively chose to create peace in a situation that could have turned violent. They demonstrated that character development isn't theoretical—it's practical preparation for real-world leadership opportunities that emerge without warning.

The Cult of Tradition

Athletic programs are among the most resistant to change in any sector. The resistance isn't accidental—it's systematic and deeply rooted in cultural mythology about what creates champions.

I've heard the same arguments countless times:

"This is how champions are made."
 "We can't go soft now."
 "Kids today need tougher coaching, not easier treatment."

These responses reveal fundamental misunderstandings about what actually develops mental toughness and competitive excellence. Recent neuroscience research shows why traditional fear-based approaches often fail. Stress hormones negatively impact the prefrontal cortex where learning and decision-making occur[29]. The very approaches designed to create toughness actually create mental interference that prevents athletes from accessing their full potential.

The question isn't whether to have high standards. It's whether fear or support better helps athletes reach those standards.

EVIDENCE FROM OTHER COUNTRIES: What Sweden Gets Right

Research on Swedish athletes provides compelling evidence for alternative approaches. Their coaching culture emphasizes coach-athlete relationships built on mutual respect, supportive rather than punitive environments, learning-focused feedback systems, and long-term development over immediate performance demands.

Athletes in these environments consistently report more positive experiences and sustained engagement in their sports[30].

Here's what matters: Swedish athletes aren't just happier—they're successful. They compete at the highest international levels across multiple sports, earning Olympic medals, World Cup titles, and professional careers. Yet they achieve this excellence through positive development rather than fear-based motivation.

The Swedish approach demonstrates something American sports culture often resists: you don't have to choose between winning and humanity. You don't have to break people to build champions. Their athletes prove that sustainable success can emerge from environments where respect and high standards coexist, where intensity and dignity aren't opposites.

This isn't about adopting Swedish culture wholesale or pretending their model translates perfectly to

American contexts. It's about recognizing that different approaches are possible—and that some of those approaches produce both better outcomes and better human beings.

The question isn't whether other models exist. It's whether we're willing to examine ours honestly enough to consider them.

The Lies We Tell Ourselves

Myth: "If it ain't broke, don't fix it."
Reality: Most dysfunction hides in plain sight until it explodes into a crisis that damages everyone involved.

Myth: "We've always done it this way."
Reality: Tradition isn't a defense for harmful practices. Many "traditional" approaches in athletics have been proven counterproductive by decades of research.

Myth: "They'll get over it."
Reality: Trauma accumulates over time and affects performance, relationships, and life success long after athletic careers end.

Myth: "It's just part of the game."
Reality: Culture is created by choices, not inevitability. Every toxic norm was once optional and can be changed through intentional effort.

Building G.R.A.C.E Under Pressure

Through years of working with programs facing various challenges, I began to see patterns in what enabled sustainable transformation. The most successful programs shared certain characteristics, which I organized into the G.R.A.C.E framework:

Goodwill: ASSUME INTENT, CREATE GROWTH:

Start with the assumption that people want to do right, even when their behavior suggests otherwise. This doesn't mean accepting harmful actions or ignoring problems. It means approaching conflicts and challenges from a foundation of positive intent rather than suspicion and blame. It means believing that behind most "bad" behavior is someone trying to solve a problem with the limited tools they possess. Goodwill creates what psychologists call "psychological safety"environments where people feel safe to take risks, make mistakes, and be vulnerable. When we assume positive intent, we create space for honest conversations that solve root problems instead of just punishing symptoms.

Respect: DIGNITY IS STRATEGY

Treat everyone like they matter, regardless of their role, performance level, or mistakes. This includes honoring the dignity of opponents, officials, teammates, parents, and community members even during disagreements or disappointing outcomes.

Respect recognizes that everyone deserves to be treated as a human being with inherent worth that doesn't fluctuate based on performance. Players fight harder for coaches who treat them with dignity. They support teammates who make mistakes instead of joining in criticism. During a playoff game with controversial officiating, our players maintained composure and continued competing at maximum intensity because we'd practiced respect under pressure until it became automatic.

Accountability: FIX THE ROOT, NOT JUST THE RULE:

Own your choices and help others own theirs. Traditional accountability focuses on punishment: late to practice means running laps, poor behavior means benching, mistakes mean consequences designed to prevent recurrence through fear. Framework accountability focuses on problem-solving: late to practice means figuring out what's preventing punctuality and addressing it. The goal isn't permissiveness—it's getting to root causes instead of just treating symptoms.

When athletes started arriving late consistently, instead of implementing stricter penalties, we discovered that three players shared one unreliable car and had no other transportation. We connected them with teammates who lived nearby and adjusted practice start times by fifteen minutes. Punctuality improved immediately because we solved the actual problem instead of just punishing the symptom.

This approach takes more initial investment in teaching and relationship-building, but it produces lasting behavior change. Athletes develop internal motivation rather than compliance based on fear. They understand and own the reasons behind expectations instead of just following rules to avoid consequences. When accountability focuses on growth instead of punishment, people take ownership of their development.

Civility: KEEP CHARACTER WHEN IT'S HARDEST

Keep your values when the pressure's on. This involves maintaining productive communication during conflicts, competing with intensity while preserving relationships, and demonstrating that excellence and character can coexist under any circumstances.

Excellence: RAISE THE BAR, BRING EVERYONE

Get better while helping others get better. Excellence means pursuing your potential while helping others pursue theirs. This creates team chemistry that translates to competitive advantage. When everyone feels valued, everyone contributes more effectively. True excellence understands that individual greatness only matters if it serves something larger than individual glory.

What follows are real stories showing what each principle looks like when tested under fire.

GOODWILL: Seeing Beyond Suspicion

I was certain Khalil was stealing from the locker room.

Equipment kept disappearing—water bottles, towels, even some of the older players' extra shoes. Khalil was always the last one to leave practice, always hanging around when he should have been heading home. New kid, quiet, defensive when asked direct questions.

The pattern seemed obvious.

I pulled him aside after practice on a Tuesday. "Khalil, we need to talk about some missing equipment."

His whole body went rigid. "I didn't take nothing."

"I'm not accusing you. I'm asking if you've seen anything."

"Nobody ever sees me," he said, and something in his voice made me pause.

It took three more weeks to discover the truth. Khalil's younger brother had been walking home from elementary school and getting jumped by older kids who stole his backpack, his lunch money, sometimes his shoes. Khalil had been taking extra equipment to replace what his brother lost, too proud to ask for help, too ashamed to explain why an eleven-year-old kept coming home barefoot.

The day I learned this, I sat in my office and cried. Not because equipment had been stolen, but because I had seen suspicious behavior where I should have seen sacrifice. I had assumed selfishness when I was witnessing the most profound kind of love—a teenager protecting his little brother the only way he knew how.

I found Khalil before practice that evening.

"I know about your brother," I said. "And I'm sorry I didn't ask better questions."

He looked at the floor. "I was gonna bring everything back. I just needed time."

"Khalil, look at me." He did, eyes wet but defiant. "You don't need to bring anything back. But next time something like this happens, you come to me first. That's what we do here—we protect each other. That includes you."

"Why would you help me? I stole from you."

"Because you were trying to protect your brother. That tells me exactly who you are."

Goodwill means starting with the assumption that

people want to do right, even when their actions seem to suggest otherwise. It means believing that behind most "bad" behavior is someone trying to solve a problem with the limited tools they possess.

Khalil graduated as our team captain. His brother is now a sophomore on the varsity team. Sometimes the best gifts come disguised as problems we're too quick to solve.

RESPECT: Dignity in the Shadows

Maria Santos never started a game in four years of high school basketball. Five-foot-two in a sport that favors height, she possessed what coaches politely call "limited athletic ability."

But during our most important game of the season league championship, packed gymnasium, college scouts in the stands Maria taught us what dignity looks like.

We were up by twenty with two minutes left when Coach Williams finally put Maria in the game. The crowd gave her a standing ovation. She was beaming as she checked in at the scorer's table.

Thirty seconds later, she fouled out.

Hard foul, too. Knocked their best player to the ground going for a steal. The referee's whistle was immediate and sharp. Maria's basketball career was over.

Instead of hanging her head, instead of crying or apologizing, Maria walked directly to the opposing player and helped her up. "Good game," she said simply. "You've been incredible to watch all season."

Then she walked to our bench, hugged every teammate, and took her seat with the same quiet pride she'd carried for four years.

The opposing player found Maria after the game. "I've been playing basketball for eight years," she said. "That was the classiest thing I've ever seen on a court."

Maria never scored more than six points in any high school game. But she showed us that respect isn't earned through performance—it's given because someone matters. She proved that dignity doesn't depend on skill level or playing time or recognition from others.

She demonstrated that how you treat people in your final moments reveals who you really are.

ACCOUNTABILITY: Owning the Whistle

"You're losing them," Assistant Coach Courtney Miller said to me after a particularly brutal practice. "The way you're pushing, it's not working."

I was defensive immediately. "They need to be challenged. We have three weeks until playoffs."

"Challenge isn't the same as punishment. You're coaching angry, and they're playing scared."

I could feel the heat rising in my face. "So you think I should just let them coast? Is that what you're suggesting?"

Courtney didn't flinch. "I'm suggesting you remember why you started coaching in the first place. Because right now? You're becoming the kind of coach we both used to complain about."

That hit different. Because she was right. I had been taking my frustration about a difficult season out on the players. Demanding perfection instead of teaching improvement. Focusing on what they were doing wrong instead of building on what they were doing right.

"So what do you suggest?" I asked, quieter now.

"Start with an apology. Then start with encouragement. They already know what they're doing wrong, Alva. They need to remember what they're doing right."

The next day, I called the team together before practice.

"I owe you an apology," I said. "I've been coaching my frustration instead of coaching your development. That's not fair to you, and it's not effective leadership. I'm going to do better. I need you to hold me to that."

The silence was thick. Then Jasmine, our point guard, spoke up: "Coach, we're frustrated too. We want to win. We just need you to believe we can."

"I do believe you can. And I'm sorry I made you question that."

The change wasn't immediate, but it was real. Players started taking risks again instead of playing not to make mistakes. They began supporting each other instead of looking over their shoulders for criticism. The culture shifted from fear-based to growth-based.

We made it to the regional semifinals that year. More importantly, we rebuilt trust that had been damaged by my unwillingness to examine my own behavior.

Accountability means owning your choices and helping others own theirs. It means being willing to be wrong and to grow from that wrongness. It means understanding that leadership isn't about being right—it's about doing right.

CIVILITY: Leadership in the Noise

The game was spiraling toward chaos. Technical

fouls, ejections, parents screaming at officials, players from both teams talking trash that was moving beyond competitive banter into personal territory.

With four minutes left in the fourth quarter, everything that could go wrong was going wrong.

That's when Victor called timeout.

Not the official timeout—just his voice cutting through the noise, calm and clear: "Everybody take a breath."

Both teams stopped. The referees paused. Even the crowd noise dimmed.

"We're here to compete," Victor continued, looking at players from both teams. "We're not here to tear each other down. Let's finish this right."

The opposing team's captain, Marcus, stepped forward. "Man, who are you to—"

"I'm someone who's seen what happens when this gets out of control," Victor said, and something in his tone made Marcus stop. "I'm someone who knows that ten years from now, you won't remember the score. But you'll remember what kind of person you were in this moment."

One of the referees, an older man who'd been officiating for twenty years, nodded slowly. "The young man's right. Let's play basketball."

Marcus looked at Victor for a long moment, then extended his hand. "Alright. Let's finish clean."

He was eighteen years old, captain of our basketball team, talking sense into a gymnasium full of adults who had lost their perspective. His voice carried the kind of authority that comes from character rather than position.

The last four minutes of that game were played at the highest level—intense, competitive, respectful. Both teams fought hard, but they fought clean. The crowd remembered they were watching kids, not gladiators.

We lost by three points. It was one of our best losses ever.

Civility isn't weakness disguised as politeness. It's strength choosing to stay human when everything around you is losing its humanity. It's the voice that stays calm when chaos feels like the easier choice.

Victor now teaches middle school and coaches our JV team. He still has that voice—the one that remembers what matters when everyone else forgets.

EXCELLENCE: The Pass, Not the Glory

With twelve seconds left and our team down by one, everyone in the gymnasium knew the ball was going to DeShawn Martinez. Twenty-eight points, eight rebounds, the kind of night that gets written up in local newspapers and remembered in yearbooks.

The inbound pass came to DeShawn at the top of the key. Two defenders collapsed on him immediately. He could have forced the shot, probably should have, by most standards. It was his moment, his game, his chance at glory.

Instead, he saw what the defense didn't: Javon Williams, wide open in the corner. The kid who'd been struggling with his shot all season, averaging four points per game, playing because of grades rather than skill.

DeShawn's pass was perfect. Javon's shot was true. We won by two.

In the locker room afterward, DeShawn was asked why he passed up the final shot.

"Because winning mattered more than my stats," he said simply. "And because Javon needed that moment more than I did."

Excellence means pursuing your potential while helping others pursue theirs. It's understanding that individual greatness only matters if it serves something larger than individual glory.

DeShawn got a full scholarship to play Division I basketball. Javon went on to become our team manager and is now studying sports medicine. That pass connected their futures in ways neither could have imagined.

True excellence multiplies itself through others. It creates moments that matter more than any individual achievement.

G.R.A.C.E: From Theory to Court

When Victor started as a freshman, he had serious attitude problems. Defensive, quick to anger, convinced everyone was against him. Traditional approaches would have labeled him a troublemaker and either kicked him off the team or tried to break his spirit through punishment.

Instead, we assumed his defensiveness came from experience with adults who'd disappointed him (Goodwill). His anger came from being misunderstood. We gave him the benefit of the doubt while setting clear expectations.

We treated him with the same dignity we wanted for our own children (Respect), listening to his perspective and honoring his experiences even when we disagreed with his choices.

We helped him understand how his actions affected teammates and coaches (Accountability), focusing on learning rather than punishment when problems arose.

We maintained consistent expectations and communication even when he tested boundaries (Civility), showing him that relationships could survive conflict.

We challenged him to develop his potential while encouraging him to help younger players do the same (Excellence).

By senior year, Victor was the team captain who prevented the restaurant brawl by stepping between fighting players and talking them down. The young man who had arrived defensive and angry became a leader who protected others and created peace.

This is what G.R.A.C.E looks like in practice: not a one-time intervention, but a consistent approach applied over time that transforms how people see themselves and their role in the world.

Pressure Reveals. Preparation Builds.

The most powerful character development happens not during calm moments, but when pressure reveals who people really are. Athletics provides unique opportunities to practice character skills under stress, preparing young people for leadership challenges they'll face throughout their lives.

This requires intentional approaches:

Morning Check-ins: Every practice started with

two minutes focused on one principle. Not lectures—quick discussions about how to apply it that day. "Today we're focusing on goodwill. What does it look like to assume positive intent when a teammate makes a mistake?"

Pressure Point Training: Deliberately create challenging situations in practice so athletes can develop appropriate responses when stakes are low. This might involve practicing composure during poor officiating scenarios, maintaining communication during comeback attempts, or supporting teammates through mistakes in crucial moments.

Real-Time Coaching: Address character moments immediately when they occur during competition. Rather than waiting until after games to discuss behavior, provide brief feedback during timeouts or breaks that reinforces values under pressure.

Reflection and Learning: Create regular opportunities to discuss how character and performance connect. Help athletes understand that emotional regulation, team support, and respectful competition enhance rather than inhibit their ability to compete at their highest level.

When the Pushback Comes

Change is never smooth or immediate. Every program implementing systematic culture transformation faces resistance from multiple sources:

Athletes who test new boundaries
Parents who prefer familiar approaches even when they're harmful
Community members who confuse tradition with effectiveness
Even coaches who struggle to modify ingrained habits

The key is persistence guided by clear values. When Victor tested boundaries during his sophomore year, when parents questioned why we weren't "tougher" on players, when community members criticized our approaches during a difficult season, we maintained consistency in our framework while adjusting specific methods based on feedback and results.

The restaurant incident validated years of investment in character development under pressure. Those players had practiced conflict resolution, learned de-escalation techniques, and internalized values that guided their decisions when no adults were present to supervise. They became the kind of leaders who create positive change in their communities throughout their lives.

Hard-Won Truths

Character under fire isn't automatic—it's developed through systematic practice and consistent reinforcement. The programs that successfully prepare young people for real-world leadership challenges are those that understand character development requires as much attention and skill as any athletic technique.

The most important insight is that pressure reveals character, but it doesn't develop character. That development happens through daily choices, consistent modeling, and intentional practice during less stressful moments that prepare athletes for the tests that come without warning.

When the 2 AM call comes, when the pressure peaks, when the moment demands more than skill—that's when you discover whether you built character or just talked about it.

Build it now. Practice it daily. Trust it when everything's on the line.

Reflection Questions

1. **Personal Character Under Pressure:** Think about your last challenging competitive situation. How did you respond when things went wrong? Did your behavior reflect the character you claim to value?

2. **Pressure Point Identification:** What situations in your sport create the most pressure for athletes to compromise their values? How could you prepare them for those moments?

3. **Change Resistance Assessment:** What sources of resistance to character development do you face in your program? How might the G.R.A.C.E framework help address those concerns?

4. **Legacy Consideration:** What kind of leaders do you want your athletes to become in their communities? How does your current approach prepare them for that responsibility?

Chapter Assignment

Character Under Fire Development Plan: Design specific strategies for developing character skills under pressure:

Pressure Situation Analysis:

- Identify the five most challenging situations your athletes face where character is tested
- Analyze how your current program prepares athletes for these moments
- Assess gaps between your stated values and athlete behavior under pressure

G.R.A.C.E Implementation Strategy:

- Develop specific applications of each G.R.A.C.E principle to your sport and program context

- Create practice scenarios where athletes can develop character skills under controlled pressure
- Design real-time coaching strategies for reinforcing values during competition

Measurement and Adjustment Plan:

- Establish clear indicators of character development under pressure
- Create feedback systems for athletes to self-assess their character growth
- Develop long-term tracking of how your athletes demonstrate leadership in their communities

Implement one element of your plan immediately and document results over a one-month period.

Chapter 8

G.R.A.C.E Framework—How it Works

The framework requires different metrics. Competitive results alongside character development indicators are measured. We measured retention and chemistry alongside wins and losses. Athletes are surveyed about their experience and growth, not just their satisfaction with playing time or team success.

WHAT WE'VE LEARNED

Principles work synergistically—each one reinforces and strengthens the others. Goodwill creates the foundation for respect. Respect enables accountability conversations. Accountability practiced with civility builds trust. Trust allows excellence to emerge both individually and collectively.

The framework isn't perfect, and implementation isn't always smooth. But it provides clear direction when difficult decisions arise and consistent language for discussing behavior expectations across all stakeholder groups.

The most important lesson: character development is practical preparation for real-world leadership opportunities that emerge without warning. We aim to develop leaders who choose peace over violence, dignity over dominance, and community over individual glory.

That's what G.R.A.C.E does. That's what these five principles create. That's what every student in every program deserves.

Reflection Questions

1. **Principle Application:** Which of the five principles would be most challenging for your program to implement consistently? What specific obstacles would you need to address?

2. **Current Practice Assessment:** How do your current approaches to discipline, motivation, and team building align with the framework principles? Where do you see the biggest gaps?

3. **Measurement Strategy:** How would you measure success if you implemented systematic character development alongside competitive preparation? What evidence would demonstrate effectiveness?

4. **Personal Modeling:** Which principle do you personally struggle with most under pressure? How could your own development in that area improve your program's culture?

Chapter Assignment

G.R.A.C.E Implementation Pilot: Choose one principle to focus on for the next month:

Week 1: Baseline Assessment

- Document current practices related to your chosen principle
- Survey athletes about their perception of how this principle currently operates in your program
- Identify specific situations where this principle is most challenging to maintain

Week 2-3: Focused Implementation

- Modify daily practices to emphasize your chosen principle
- Create specific language and expectations around this principle
- Address challenges and resistance as they arise

Week 4: Evaluation and Planning

- Assess changes in behavior, attitude, and program culture
- Gather feedback from athletes, coaches, and parents about observed differences
- Plan for expanding implementation to additional principles based on lessons learned

Document your experience and results to inform broader program transformation planning.

Chapter 9

Understanding Where People Stand—The Culture Map

NICE KIDS FINISH LAST?

During warm-ups before rivalry games, our team captains routinely helped opposing players who stumbled during drills. These small gestures spoke volumes about program culture and demonstrated that competitive intensity could coexist with respect for opponents.

But as players returned to their teammates, parents in the stands shook their heads in disapproval. "These kids are too soft," I heard one father tell another. "That's not how you get ready for battle."

This illustrates the persistent gap between attitude and behavior that complicates culture change efforts. The players' actions reflected values we'd been developing systematically. The parents' attitudes remained rooted in zero-sum thinking where helping opponents somehow weakened their own children's chances for success.

Understanding this gap is crucial for effective transformation. People can demonstrate appropriate behavior while harboring resentful attitudes that emerge when tested. Others genuinely value positive principles but lack skills to express them consistently when emotions run high.

THE CULTURE MAP: ATTITUDE VS. BEHAVIOR

Through years of working with various stakeholders,

I've observed four distinct patterns in how people approach civility and character development:

HOSTILE (Negative Attitude + Negative Behavior)

These individuals believe incivility is justified and act accordingly. They think intimidation enhances performance, that respect makes athletes weak, and that winning requires abandoning character when necessary.

Example: The parent who screams at officials during every game, believing this demonstrates care for their child and might influence future calls. They're not just misbehaving—they're convinced their behavior is appropriate.

COMPLIANT (Negative Attitude + Positive Behavior)

These people act appropriately but harbor resentful attitudes underneath surface cooperation. They follow rules because they have to, not because they believe in the values behind them.

Example: The coach who speaks respectfully to athletes when administrators are present but ridicules players privately or during away games. They understand expectations but don't embrace the philosophy.

INCONSISTENT (Positive Attitude + Negative Behavior)

These individuals genuinely value civility but lack skills to express these values consistently when stressed. They mean well but haven't developed the emotional regulation or communication techniques needed to maintain standards when everything's falling apart.

Example: The athletic director who believes strongly in positive culture but loses composure during budget meetings with hostile board members, undermining their credibility with the same behavior they prohibit in their programs.

CHAMPION (Positive Attitude + Positive Behavior)

These people both value civility principles and have developed skills to practice them consistently, even under extreme stress. They understand that character and competence strengthen each other.

Example: The team captain who maintains encouraging communication with struggling teammates during playoff losses, demonstrates respect toward opponents who are trash-talking, and helps younger players develop both skills and character throughout the season.

WHY PEOPLE RESIST THE CULTURE YOU'RE

BUILDING

Understanding why people operate from negative attitudes or demonstrate inconsistent behavior helps in developing targeted interventions:

Fear-Based Thinking: Many people believe showing respect will be perceived as weakness, that others are gaining unfair advantages through unsportsmanlike behavior, or that their athletes will be taken advantage of if they don't respond aggressively.

Scarcity Mindset: The belief that success is limited creates zero-sum thinking where another team's victory diminishes your own worth, where helping opponents somehow hurts your chances, or where resources and opportunities are finite rather than expandable.

Cultural Conditioning: "That's how we've always done things" gets reinforced by media that glamorizes aggressive behavior, communities that celebrate results regardless of methods, and traditions that prioritize wins over development.

Lack of Skills: Many people have never learned healthy ways to express intensity, handle disappointment constructively, resolve conflicts without personal attacks, or maintain relationships through disagreements.

Systemic Rewards: Programs that overlook bad behavior from talented athletes, communities that celebrate results while ignoring methods, and organizations that promote based on wins rather than values create environments where civility appears disadvantageous.

MOVING PEOPLE TO THE RIGHT SIDE OF THE MAP

Hostile → Compliant: Behavior Change First

With people who believe incivility is justified, focus on changing behavior before attempting to change attitudes. Clear expectations, consistent consequences, and gradual education about the effectiveness of positive approaches can eventually shift both behavior and underlying beliefs. Don't expect immediate attitude change, but insist on behavioral compliance. Over time, people who experience better results through civil behavior often begin to question their previous assumptions.

Compliant → Champion: Attitude Development

For people who comply behaviorally but remain resentful, focus on education about why civility enhances rather than inhibits performance. Share research, provide examples of successful programs that prioritize character, and create opportunities for them to experience positive results personally. Address underlying fears and misconceptions. Help them understand that respect and intensity can coexist, that character development produces better athletes.

Inconsistent → Champion: Skill Development

People who value civility but struggle with consistent application need practical training in emotional regulation, communication techniques, and conflict resolution. They have the right intentions but lack the tools to express them effectively when stressed. Provide specific techniques for maintaining composure, practice opportunities in low-stakes situations, and ongoing coaching to help them develop competency alongside commitment.

WHO INFLUENCES CULTURE MOST?

Understanding where people stand helps predict their influence on program culture. Champions naturally become culture carriers who model and teach others. Inconsistent people can become champions with proper development. Compliant individuals might influence others negatively despite following rules themselves. Hostile people actively undermine positive culture and require immediate attention.

The goal isn't to have everyone start as champions—it's to move everyone toward championship thinking and behavior over time. Programs that understand this process can develop targeted strategies for working with different stakeholder groups rather than using one-size-fits-all approaches that fail to address underlying attitudes and skill gaps.

Champions don't just behave well—they actively shape the environment around them. They call out problems early, support struggling teammates, and create peer accountability that makes negative behavior socially costly. One champion can influence fifteen people. One hostile person can poison thirty.

That's why identifying and developing champions is the most strategic investment any program can make.

BUILDING A PROGRAM FULL OF CHAMPIONS

Assessment First: Regular evaluation of where key stakeholders stand provides information needed for targeted interventions. Anonymous surveys, behavioral observation, and one-on-one conversations reveal attitudes and skill levels that inform development planning.

Match Strategy to Starting Point: Hostile individuals need clear boundaries and gradual exposure to positive alternatives. Compliant people need education about the benefits of genuine commitment. Inconsistent individuals need skill development and practice opportunities. Champions need leadership roles and mentorship responsibilities.

Create Momentum: As more people move toward championship attitudes and behaviors, program culture shifts in positive directions. Champions influence others through modeling and peer accountability, creating momentum that eventually makes positive culture the norm rather than the exception.

Support the Journey: Programs that successfully develop champions provide ongoing education, skill development opportunities, recognition for positive growth, and accountability for continued development. Championship thinking and behavior require cultivation, not just expectation.

FINAL NOTE: FEAR WEARS MANY JERSEYS

Most resistance to positive culture change comes from fear rather than malice. People worry that civility will make their athletes less competitive, that respect will be perceived as weakness, or that positive approaches won't work in high-stakes situations.

The most effective strategy is demonstrating rather than just explaining. When people see civil competitors performing better when it matters most, when they observe respectful programs achieving lasting success, when they experience positive results personally, their attitudes begin to shift naturally.

Fear doesn't argue with results. It just finds new excuses until those run out too.

Reflection Questions

1. **Self-Assessment:** Where do you typically operate under normal conditions versus high-pressure situations? What triggers cause you to migrate toward less civil responses?

2. **Stakeholder Analysis:** Which category best describes the key people in your program (athletes, coaches, parents, administrators)? What evidence supports your assessment?

3. **Development Planning:** What specific interventions would most effectively help your stakeholders move toward championship attitudes and behaviors?

4. **Influence Mapping:** Who in your program currently operates as champions who could help influence others? How could you better utilize their positive impact?

Chapter Assignment

Stakeholder Culture Mapping: Create a comprehensive assessment of where key people in your program currently stand:

Individual Assessment:

- Survey athletes, coaches, parents, and administrators using behavioral and attitudinal indicators
- Conduct confidential interviews with representative stakeholders from each group
- Observe behavior during both routine and high-pressure situations

Analysis and Planning:

- Map stakeholders into the four categories based on your assessment data
- Identify patterns and trends within each stakeholder group
- Develop targeted intervention strategies for moving people toward championship thinking and behavior
- Create timeline and accountability measures for culture development efforts

Implementation Strategy:

- Begin with willing champions who can model and influence others
- Address hostile behavior immediately while providing education and support
- Develop skills training for inconsistent individuals who want to improve
- Create recognition and incentive systems that reward movement toward championship attitudes and behaviors

Document your findings and begin implementation with highest-priority interventions.

Chapter 10

Assessing Culture—Measuring What Matters

WHAT YOU CAN'T SEE CAN HURT YOU

Three months into my first year as athletic director, a fellow athletic director thought his program was healthy. They were winning games, parents seemed satisfied, and he received few complaints. The surface looked fine.

Then a senior athlete's mother requested a private meeting.

"My daughter loves volleyball, but she's going to quit after this season."

"Why? She's one of our best players."

"Because she can't take the locker room culture anymore. The seniors have been bullying the younger girls all season. Making them do homework, cleaning up after them, calling them names. My daughter reported it twice, but nothing changed."

He was shocked. He walked past that locker room daily, observed practices, talked with athletes regularly. How had I missed systematic bullying happening right under my nose?

That conversation taught me the most important lesson of my administrative career: absence of visible problems doesn't equal presence of healthy culture.

WHY SCOREBOARDS AND SURVEYS AREN'T ENOUGH

Most programs measure what's easy to count rather than what actually matters:

Surface Metrics: Win-loss records, participation numbers, scholarship recipients, and championship banners tell us about outcomes but nothing about the process that created them or whether that process is sustainable.

Crisis Indicators: Waiting for formal complaints or disciplinary incidents means intervening after damage has already occurred to athletes, families, and program reputation.

Adult Perspectives Only: Surveys often focus on parent and coach satisfaction while missing athlete experiences—the most important indicators of program health.

Annual Assessment: Once-yearly evaluations miss patterns that develop over time and provide information too late for meaningful intervention during current seasons.

The metrics that predict long-term success are harder to capture but far more important: whether athletes feel psychologically safe with teammates, how coaches are developing character alongside skills, whether the competitive environment builds resilience or creates trauma, and what impact participation has on young people's lives beyond athletics.

THREE LEVELS OF CULTURE ASSESSMENT

Effective culture assessment requires multiple approaches that capture different perspectives and measure various aspects of program environment.

LEVEL 1: WHAT PEOPLE SAY (Perceptions & Experience)

For Athletes:

- "I feel respected and valued by my coaches, regardless of my playing time"
- "My teammates support each other both on and off the field"
- "I can express concerns or ask questions without fear of retaliation"
- "This program is helping me develop life skills beyond athletics"
- "I feel emotionally safe in this environment, even when making mistakes"

For Coaches:

- "I feel supported by administration in addressing behavioral issues"
- "Parents in this program generally trust and support coaching decisions"
- "I can focus on teaching and development rather than managing drama"

- "I'm proud to be associated with this program's reputation"

For Parents:

- "Communication from coaches and administration is clear and timely"
- "My child is treated fairly and with dignity in this program"
- "The competitive environment is challenging but supportive"
- "This program represents values I want my child to learn"

For Officials:

- "Coaches, players, and spectators treat me with respect during games"
- "I feel safe officiating games in this program/league"
- "Program leadership supports officials and addresses inappropriate behavior"

LEVEL 2: WHAT PEOPLE DO (Observable Behavior)

Positive Indicators:

- Athletes encouraging teammates during mistakes rather than showing frustration
- Coaches providing constructive feedback that builds rather than tears down
- Parents supporting program decisions even when disappointed with individual outcomes

- Community members attending events to support rather than criticize young people

Warning Signs:

- Increased conflicts requiring administrative intervention
- Athletes withdrawing from team activities or quitting mid-season without clear reasons
- Parents forming negative coalitions or frequently questioning program decisions
- Officials reporting concerns about spectator or participant behavior

LEVEL 3: WHAT ENDURES (Long-Term Impact)

Alumni Feedback:

- What life skills did you learn through athletics that you still use today?
- How did your athletic experience influence your leadership style and character?
- What do you remember most about your time in the program?
- Would you want your children to have similar athletic experiences?

Community Impact:

- Leadership roles assumed by former athletes in their communities
- Continued involvement in athletics as coaches, officials, or volunteers

- Success in academic, career, and relationship areas that correlate with character development

HOW TO RUN A CULTURE AUDIT

Phase 1: Baseline Measurement

Start with anonymous online surveys ensuring confidentiality and high participation rates. Segment responses by role, sport, and tenure for comparison analysis. Use professional survey platforms that enable honest feedback without fear of retaliation.

Phase 2: Qualitative Data Collection

Conduct separate focus groups for athletes, parents, coaches, and officials using structured discussion guides that cover specific culture dimensions. Professional facilitation ensures psychological safety and produces actionable insights rather than just complaints or praise.

Phase 3: Behavioral Observation

Document actual behavior during practices, games, and program events. Look for consistency between stated values and demonstrated actions. Pay attention to behavior during high-pressure situations when character is most tested.

Phase 4: Analysis and Action Planning

Identify patterns across different data sources and stakeholder groups. Distinguish between isolated incidents and systematic problems. Develop targeted interventions based on specific findings rather than general assumptions.

Common Assessment Challenges

Resistance to Honest Feedback: Some participants may fear negative consequences from honest assessment, leading to artificially positive results that don't reflect reality. Address this by ensuring genuine anonymity, communicating how feedback will be used constructively rather than punitively, and modeling openness to feedback at leadership levels.

Data Overwhelm: Comprehensive assessment can generate more information than programs can effectively process. Focus on key indicators that align with specific improvement goals, use simple reporting formats that highlight actionable insights, and provide training in data interpretation and action planning.

Implementation Without Assessment: Some programs want to implement changes without measuring current state or progress, leading to unfocused efforts and unclear results. Emphasize that assessment enables rather than hinders improvement and demonstrate how successful programs use data to achieve better outcomes.

Assessment Without Implementation: Other programs conduct extensive assessment but fail to act on results, leading to stakeholder cynicism about the value of providing feedback. Commit to action planning and implementation before beginning assessment and provide regular updates on progress.

WHERE GOOD DATA GOES TO DIE

Too Much, Too Late

Some programs conduct extensive assessment but fail to act on results, leading to stakeholder cynicism about the value of providing feedback. Commit to action planning and implementation before beginning assessment. Provide regular updates on progress. Data without action is worse than no data at all—it teaches people their voices don't matter.

Asking Without Listening

Resistance to honest feedback creates artificially positive results that don't reflect reality. Address this by ensuring genuine anonymity, communicating how feedback will be used constructively rather than punitively, and modeling openness to feedback at leadership levels. If people think honesty will cost them, they'll tell you what you want to hear instead of what you need to know.

Survey Fatigue is Real

Comprehensive assessment can generate more information than programs can effectively process. Focus on key indicators that align with specific improvement goals. Use simple reporting formats that highlight actionable insights. Provide training in data interpretation and action planning. Quality beats quantity every time.

MAKE ASSESSMENT A HABIT, NOT A HEADLINE

Successful programs integrate assessment into regular operations rather than treating it as an additional burden:

Ongoing Feedback Systems: Create multiple opportunities for stakeholders to provide input throughout the year rather than just annual surveys. Include brief culture check-ins during team meetings, parent conversations, and coach evaluations.

Real-Time Adjustment: Use assessment information to make immediate improvements rather than waiting for comprehensive analysis. If feedback reveals communication problems, address them immediately rather than waiting until next season.

Stakeholder Involvement: Include representatives from different stakeholder groups in assessment design and analysis to ensure relevant questions and accurate interpretation of results.

Transparency and Communication: Share appropriate assessment results with stakeholders and explain how feedback is being used to improve program culture. This builds trust and encourages continued honest participation in evaluation processes.

CULTURE WHISPERS BEFORE IT SHOUTS

The most valuable assessment information often comes from informal conversations and careful observation rather than formal surveys. Athletes will share concerns during casual interactions that they wouldn't put on an evaluation form. Parents will reveal their true feelings during sideline conversations that official feedback systems miss.

Pay attention to patterns rather than individual complaints or praise. When several people independently identify the same concern, it usually represents a systematic issue requiring attention.

The volleyball player's mother who came to my office wasn't the first person to notice the bullying. She was just the first person who felt safe enough to name it directly. The whispers had been there for months—athletes showing up late, withdrawing from team activities, parents having hushed conversations in parking lots after practice.

Culture problems rarely announce themselves. They accumulate in small moments: the joke that goes too far, the comment that stings but gets dismissed as "just teasing," the pattern of exclusion that becomes normalized because no one intervenes.

Your job isn't just to measure culture. It's to listen for the whispers before they become screams.

Reflection Questions

1. **Current Assessment Gap:** What aspects of your program culture are you not currently measuring that might reveal important information about stakeholder experiences?

2. **Feedback Environment:** Is your program psychologically safe enough for stakeholders to provide honest feedback, or would you need to address trust issues first?

3. **Implementation Capacity:** Do you have the leadership commitment, resources, and expertise needed to act on assessment findings effectively?

4. **Communication Strategy:** How would you communicate assessment results and improvement plans to build confidence rather than create panic or negative publicity?

Chapter Assignment

Comprehensive Culture Assessment Design:
Develop and implement a multi-level assessment of your program culture:

Assessment Planning:

- Design surveys for each stakeholder group using questions appropriate to their perspective and role
- Plan focus groups or individual interviews with representative participants from each group
- Create observation protocols for documenting behavior during practices, games, and program events
- Establish timeline and communication plan for assessment implementation

Data Collection:

- Implement surveys using anonymous platforms that ensure honest participation
- Conduct interviews and focus groups with professional facilitation if possible
- Document behavioral observations over multiple events and situations
- Gather existing data about participation rates, retention, and program outcomes

Analysis and Action Planning:

- Analyze results to identify patterns, strengths, and areas for improvement

- Compare findings across different stakeholder groups and data sources
- Develop specific, actionable improvement strategies based on assessment results
- Create timeline and accountability measures for implementing changes

Communication and Follow-Up:

- Share appropriate results with stakeholders and explain how feedback will be used
- Implement highest-priority improvements immediately
- Establish ongoing assessment systems for tracking progress over time
- Plan follow-up evaluation to measure effectiveness of culture development efforts

Chapter 11

Building Skills That Last—Character Competencies

Four Essential Competencies
THE FOUR COMPETENCIES EVERY ATHLETE NEEDS

The four core competencies that consistently appear in people who maintain character under pressure and create positive influence in their communities.

CONTINUOUS LEARNING: TURNING FEEDBACK INTO FUEL

The willingness to seek feedback, adapt to new situations, and grow from challenges rather than being defeated by them. This includes:

- Approaching mistakes as learning opportunities
- Actively soliciting input from coaches and teammates
- Remaining curious about improvement rather than defensive about criticism
- Viewing setbacks as information rather than indictments of worth

SOCIAL INTELLIGENCE: READING THE ROOM, LEADING THE TEAM

The ability to read interpersonal dynamics, communicate effectively under pressure, and influence others in positive directions. This involves:

- Understanding emotional cues from teammates and opponents

- Adapting communication style to different personalities and situations
- Managing conflicts before they damage relationships
- Motivating others through encouragement rather than criticism or fear

SYSTEMS THINKING: SEEING THE RIPPLE EFFECT

Understanding how individual actions affect team chemistry and long-term program culture. This includes:

- Recognizing how personal choices impact teammates' ability to succeed
- Considering long-term consequences rather than just immediate outcomes
- Understanding the connection between team culture and competitive performance
- Making decisions that strengthen rather than weaken program values

CULTURAL COMPETENCE: WINNING WITH DIFFERENCE

Working effectively with people from different backgrounds and creating inclusive environments where everyone can contribute their best efforts. This involves:

- Appreciating diverse perspectives and communication styles

- Avoiding assumptions based on stereotypes or limited experience
- Adapting leadership approaches to work effectively with different individuals
- Creating team traditions that honor rather than exclude differences

---

PRACTICE, DON'T PREACH

When Victor started as a freshman with "attitude problems," his first response to any feedback was defensiveness or anger. He interpreted coaching as criticism and suggestions as personal attacks. Traditional approaches would have labeled him uncoachable and either kicked him off the team or tried to break his resistance through punishment.

Instead, we focused on developing his learning mindset. We helped him understand that feedback was investment, not attack. We showed him that leaders are learners, not people who already know everything.

This looked like asking "What did you notice about that play?" before telling him what we saw. It involved celebrating his questions rather than just his correct answers. We acknowledged when he taught us something through his perspective or experience.

By senior year, Victor was actively seeking feedback from coaches, asking teammates for input on his leadership style, and using game film to identify improvement opportunities rather than just highlight successful plays. He had developed competency in learning that he could apply to academics, future careers, and relationships throughout his life.

Social intelligence developed through systematic practice, not lectures. We taught athletes to read body language and emotional cues—noticing when teammates were frustrated or discouraged before those emotions affected performance. We helped leaders understand that different people respond to different approaches. Some need encouragement, others need challenge. Some prefer direct feedback, others need time to process.

During a frustrating practice when several players weren't giving full effort, I stopped and drew circles on a whiteboard. "This is our team," I said, connecting the circles with lines. "When one person doesn't give full effort, what happens to everyone else's energy and preparation?"

Players began understanding that individual choices affect everyone's experience and performance. **Systems thinking meant considering the broader impact of personal decisions, not just immediate personal outcomes.** We taught them to see the ripple effects—how today's attitudes influenced next week's chemistry, how personal goals could either strengthen or weaken team success.

Cultural competence built through direct engagement with difference. Our teams included athletes from diverse backgrounds—different races, economic situations, family structures, and cultural traditions. Instead of ignoring differences, we addressed them directly through "Culture Share Days" where team members shared food, music, or traditions that reflected their identity and family heritage.

The result wasn't forced integration—it was genuine appreciation for difference that strengthened team unity. Athletes learned that diversity enhanced rather than threatened team chemistry when approached with respect and curiosity.

COACHING FOR COMPETENCY

Competency development doesn't happen by accident. It requires deliberate design and consistent reinforcement.

Deliberate Practice Opportunities: Rather than hoping competencies would develop naturally through participation, we created specific situations where athletes could practice character skills in controlled environments before applying them in high-pressure competitions. Scrimmages with intentionally poor officiating to practice emotional regulation. Time-pressure scenarios to practice supporting teammates through mistakes. Leadership rotations to give everyone opportunities to practice influence skills.

Real-Time Coaching: When competency moments arose during practices or games, we addressed them immediately rather than waiting for post-event discussions. Brief timeouts or halftime conversations reinforced skill development when emotions were engaged and learning was most relevant.

Reflection and Application: Regular team meetings included discussions about how competency development connected to both athletic performance and life preparation. We helped athletes understand the transferable value of character skills—how conflict resolution in the locker room prepared them for workplace challenges, how systems thinking in basketball translated to business decisions, how cultural competence on the team served their professional futures.

Leadership Rotation: Multiple athletes had opportunities to practice competency-based leadership rather than just relying on natural personality or talent-based captaincy. This ensured broader development and program sustainability. When the stars graduated, culture continued because fifteen people had practiced leadership, not just two captains.

WHEN SKILLS COMBINE

The real power comes from developing all four

competencies simultaneously. They don't work in isolation—they multiply each other's effectiveness.

Adaptive Leadership (Learning + Social Intelligence): Leaders who could adjust their approaches based on feedback and changing circumstances while maintaining positive relationships and influence. They read the room, tried new approaches, learned what worked, and refined their leadership style based on results rather than just repeating what felt comfortable.

Strategic Influence (Social Intelligence + Systems Thinking): The ability to create positive change that spread throughout the program rather than just affecting immediate relationships or situations. These athletes understood which actions would create ripple effects, how to influence culture rather than just individual behavior, and how to build momentum toward team goals.

Inclusive Excellence (Systems Thinking + Cultural Competence): Understanding how to leverage diverse perspectives and backgrounds to create team chemistry that enhanced rather than limited competitive performance. These leaders saw diversity as competitive advantage, not obstacle to overcome. They built unity through appreciation of difference rather than requiring conformity.

Evolving Wisdom (Cultural Competence + Continuous Learning): The willingness to grow in understanding and effectiveness when working with people from different backgrounds and experiences.

These athletes never stopped learning about themselves and others. They recognized that true wisdom meant knowing how much they still didn't know.

WHAT LASTS BEYOND THE GAME

The most meaningful validation came years later when former athletes contacted me about how competency development had influenced their adult lives.

They were using conflict resolution skills in workplace situations. Demonstrating cultural competence in diverse professional environments. Applying systems thinking to business and community challenges. Maintaining learning orientations that served their career advancement.

A former point guard who now manages a team of forty employees told me: "Everything I learned about reading people and adapting my communication style—that was on your court during film sessions. I use those same skills every day now, just in different jerseys."

A center who struggled with learning disabilities in high school but became a special education teacher said: "You taught me that feedback was investment, not attack. That changed how I saw myself as a learner. Now I teach my students the same thing."

Victor returned to our community as a teacher and coach, telling me, "I want to help other young people develop these same skills that changed my life trajectory." The competencies he learned through athletics became the foundation for positive influence he created throughout his adult life.

These weren't just good athletes who became successful adults. They were people who learned transferable skills through athletics that they applied to every area of their lives—parenting, careers, community leadership, relationships. The competencies we developed on courts and fields equipped them for challenges we couldn't have predicted when they were teenagers.

FINAL LESSON: COMPETENCIES ARE TRAINED, NOT HOPED FOR

Competency development requires as much systematic attention as any athletic skill. Just as we wouldn't expect athletes to develop physical techniques without instruction and practice, we can't expect character competencies to emerge automatically through participation.

The key insight is that competencies strengthen both individual performance and team chemistry. Athletes who develop social intelligence communicate better under pressure. Those who practice systems thinking make decisions that benefit team success. Cultural competence creates chemistry that becomes a competitive advantage.

Character competencies aren't soft skills that compete with competitive excellence. They're performance skills that enable it. The athletes who master these competencies don't just win more games—they build better lives.

Reflection Questions

1. **Personal Competency Assessment:** Which of the four competencies represents your strongest area, and which requires the most development? How does this affect your leadership effectiveness?

2. **Program Integration:** How could you systematically develop these competencies in your athletes rather than hoping they emerge naturally through participation?

3. **Transfer Potential:** What evidence would demonstrate that athletes are applying these competencies in academic, social, and family situations beyond athletics?

4. **Long-term Impact:** What would it mean for your community if your program consistently developed young people with strong character competencies who became positive leaders in their adult lives?

Chapter Assignment

Competency Development Implementation:
Design and implement systematic character skill development in your program:

Current State Assessment:

- Evaluate your athletes' current competency levels in each of the four areas using observation and brief conversations
- Identify which competencies would most benefit your team chemistry and competitive performance
- Analyze opportunities within your existing program structure for competency development practice

Systematic Development Plan:

- Create specific practice opportunities for each competency within regular training activities
- Design real-time coaching approaches for addressing competency moments during competitions
- Develop reflection and discussion formats that help athletes understand transfer value of character skills

Implementation and Measurement:

- Begin with one competency focus for one month, documenting changes in behavior and team chemistry
- Gradually expand to include all four competencies with specific application opportunities
- Track both athletic performance and character development indicators to demonstrate integration effectiveness
- Create feedback systems that help athletes self-assess their competency growth over time

Long-term Sustainability:

- Train multiple coaches and team leaders in competency development approaches
- Build character skill development into recruitment, team selection, and recognition systems
- Create alumni feedback opportunities to understand lasting impact of competency development
- Document successful practices for program continuity during leadership transitions

Chapter 12

Implementation—Building Your Program

WHEN THE WORST BECOMES THE CATALYST

Dr. James Patterson from State University called about Victor's application to their Master's in Education program.

"His essay about how trauma led him to understand the power of sports to heal communities is remarkable," Dr. Patterson said. "His recommendations describe character development that's rare in someone his age. We'd like to discuss bringing these approaches to our teacher preparation program."

After we hung up, I sat in my office and reflected with gratitude, but from overwhelming gratitude that the worst night of my career had become the catalyst for transformation touching thousands of young lives.

Victor had written about learning conflict resolution skills through athletics that he now used to help middle school students resolve peer disputes. He described developing cultural competence through team diversity that prepared him for working with families from different backgrounds. He explained how learning accountability through sports mistakes helped him take ownership of his professional development and teaching effectiveness.

The victim of violence had become an advocate for transformation, demonstrating the long-term impact that systematic culture development creates when implemented with consistency and commitment.

This chapter is about how you create that transformation in your program—not through wishful thinking, but through deliberate, systematic implementation that turns principles into practice.

THE 90-DAY GAME PLAN

Based on organizational change research showing that behavioral changes require 8-12 weeks of consistent practice to become automatic[31], I developed a structured approach that programs can adapt to their specific contexts and challenges.

DAYS 1–14: LAYING THE FOUNDATION

During the initial phase, focus on establishing clear expectations and communication systems while beginning immediate integration of principles into daily operations.

Assess honestly. Use the tools from Chapter 10 to understand where you actually are, not where you hope you are. The volleyball player's mother taught me that what we don't see can destroy us. Look hard at what's happening in your locker rooms, in your parent sections, in the moments when you're not watching.

Introduce the framework. Talk to all stakeholders—athletes, parents, coaches, officials—through meetings, written materials, and informal conversations. Don't lecture. Share stories. Explain why this matters. Address questions and resistance openly rather than avoiding or dismissing concerns.

Start immediately. Begin daily integration practices that require minimal time but create immediate cultural impact:

- Start each practice with a two-minute principle check-in focusing on one area per day
- Use principle language in all communication with athletes, parents, and community members
- Apply principle lens to handling mistakes, conflicts, and pressure situations
- Celebrate specific examples when stakeholders demonstrate principle-based behavior

I remember the first week we started this work. A parent who'd been screaming at referees for three seasons approached me after a game. "Coach told us this week that how we act in the stands teaches our kids more than what happens on the court," she said. "I never thought about it that way before. I'm going to do better."

Small shifts. Daily language. Consistent modeling. That's how foundation gets built.

DAYS 15–42: BUILDING SKILLS INTO HABITS

The middle phase focuses on consistent application, systematic skill development, and immediate problem-solving using the framework approach.

Train your staff. Transform traditional coaching methods to incorporate systematic principles. Practice appropriate responses to common pressure situations like poor officiating, athlete mistakes, and parent complaints before they happen in competition.

This is where you integrate new communication patterns and conflict resolution approaches into daily practice.

Change how you talk so kids can hear.
Traditional feedback often creates defensiveness because it focuses on what's wrong rather than how to improve.

Traditional: "You're not trying hard enough. You keep making the same mistakes. You need to focus better."

Framework-Enhanced: "I noticed great effort on that defensive play. Let's work on keeping that same energy when you're tired, because your leadership makes a difference for the whole team, and I want to help you be successful in those crucial moments."

The difference isn't just semantic—it's neurological. Enhanced feedback activates learning centers rather than threat responses, enabling athletes to process information more effectively.

Shift from punishment to problem-solving.
When arguments arise between athletes, the old way was to separate them, determine who was wrong, assign punishment, and move on.

The systematic approach brings arguing athletes together to understand root causes, address underlying needs, practice better communication techniques, and connect the resolution to team chemistry and performance.

Result: Skill development that prevents future problems rather than temporary peace that leaves underlying issues unresolved.

I watched this transformation happen with two seniors who'd been best friends since middle school but started clashing during their final season. The old me would have separated them, maybe benched one to "send a message." Instead, we brought them together.

"What's really happening here?" I asked.

It took twenty minutes, but we discovered the conflict wasn't about basketball—it was about one girl feeling abandoned because the other had a new boyfriend and wasn't making time for their friendship. Once we named the real problem, they could solve it. They finished the season stronger than ever and are still close friends today.

That's what happens when you build problem-solving skills instead of just enforcing compliance.

Establish feedback mechanisms. Create regular ways to identify what's working and what needs adjustment. Document early wins and lessons learned. This isn't about perfection—it's about progress.

DAYS 43–90: LOCKING IN CULTURE

The final phase emphasizes making new behaviors automatic, addressing persistent challenges systematically, and planning for long-term sustainability.

Make it automatic. Framework integration should no longer require conscious effort in all program activities. It should be how you operate, not what you're trying to operate.

Address persistent challenges. Some people will still resist. Some situations will still test you. Use systematic problem-solving rather than reactive crisis management. Go back to your principles. Trust the process.

Plan for sustainability. This is where you begin thinking about policy integration, staff training, and community partnership development. How does this work continue when you're not in the room? When you're not the coach anymore? When the resistant parent becomes a board member?

Evaluate and refine. Gather comprehensive feedback from all stakeholder groups. What's working? What needs adjustment? Culture development isn't one-and-done—it's continuous improvement.

OVERCOMING THE PUSHBACK

Every program implementing systematic culture transformation faces resistance. Here's how to address the most common objections:

"We Don't Have Time" → Integrate, Don't Add

Start by modifying existing activities rather than adding new requirements. Transform team meetings into character discussions. Integrate principles into existing practice routines. Apply framework lens to current communication with parents and officials.

Research from McKinsey & Company shows that time invested in culture development actually increases efficiency by reducing time spent managing problems[32]. Programs that invest early in systematic approaches spend less time later dealing with crises, conflicts, and relationship problems.

"This Will Hurt Our Edge" → Wooden Proved Otherwise

UCLA's John Wooden won 10 NCAA championships in 12 years using character-based coaching principles. Research consistently shows that programs focused on character development often maintain or improve competitive performance because positive cultures enhance team chemistry, reduce distractions, and enable better decision-making under pressure[33].

Track both character indicators and competitive performance to demonstrate that systematic culture development enhances rather than detracts from success.

"Parents Won't Support This" → They Already Do

National Parent Teacher Association research shows that 89% of parents consider character development as important as academic achievement[34]. Most resistance comes from misunderstanding rather than fundamental disagreement with values.

Educate parents about how character serves their children's long-term success. Show research connecting emotional regulation, leadership skills, and positive relationships to academic, career, and life outcomes. Provide specific ways parents can support systematic development at home.

"We've Tried Before" → Why This Time is Different

Most previous efforts failed because they focused on surface behaviors rather than systematic approaches, attempted to change everything simultaneously, relied on external programs rather than developing internal capacity, or lacked consistent leadership commitment.

The systematic framework succeeds because it provides comprehensive approaches rather than piecemeal programs, commits to 18-24 month implementation timelines for sustainable change, integrates character development into all program operations, and builds internal expertise rather than relying solely on external consultants.

BUILDING SYSTEMS THAT OUTLAST YOU

Long-term success requires systems that continue regardless of leadership changes, competitive pressures, or community challenges.

Policy Integration: Include character competencies in coach job descriptions and performance evaluations. Embed culture indicators in budget decisions and resource allocation priorities. Align recognition systems to celebrate character development alongside competitive achievement. Create succession planning that prioritizes culture continuity during leadership transitions.

Leadership Development: Identify and train multiple people who can model and teach systematic principles. Create mentoring relationships between experienced culture carriers and new staff members. Establish leadership development programs that prepare athletes for positive influence roles. Build alumni networks that support current programs and provide ongoing accountability.

Community Integration: Build relationships with school administrators and board members who understand the connection between athletics and character development. Engage local businesses and community organizations through partnerships that reinforce positive values. Create recognition opportunities for community members who model and support program principles.

MEASURING WHAT REALLY MATTERS

Programs that successfully implement systematic approaches track multiple indicators rather than just competitive outcomes:

Academic Performance: Research suggests positive correlations between character-based athletic programs and improved academic outcomes for student-athletes[35]. Athletes who learn accountability, goal-setting, and perseverance through sports often transfer these skills to classroom success.

Social-Emotional Development: Better conflict resolution abilities, improved teamwork and communication skills, greater resilience during challenges, and enhanced leadership capacity both within athletics and in broader school and community settings.

Long-Term Outcomes: While comprehensive research is still developing, preliminary evidence suggests benefits for college completion rates, employment success, relationship quality, and community involvement among former participants in character-focused programs.

Character Transfer: The most meaningful success indicator is evidence that athletes apply principles learned through sports to academic, family, and community situations, demonstrating that development transcends athletic participation.

YOUR FIRST SEASON BLUEPRINT

This Week: Assess current program culture honestly using tools from Chapter 10. Don't sugarcoat it. Don't explain it away. Just look at what's really happening and commit to making it better.

This Month: Create written expectations based on systematic principles and train key staff in principle-based communication. Establish feedback systems that track culture alongside performance.

This Season: Implement systematic approaches consistently across all program activities. Address challenges using principle-based problem-solving rather than reactive crisis management. Document successes and lessons learned.

This Year: Evaluate overall transformation using comprehensive assessment from multiple stakeholder perspectives. Refine approaches based on results. Share successful strategies with other programs. Develop internal expertise to continue this work long-term.

THE RIPPLE EFFECT

The most significant validation of systematic implementation comes through long-term impact on participants' lives and communities. Former athletes become coaches, teachers, business leaders, and community members who carry forward principles learned through athletics.

Research from the Search Institute shows that young people who experience strong adult relationships, high expectations, and meaningful opportunities are more likely to become successful, contributing adults[36]. Athletic programs have unique opportunities to provide these developmental experiences through systematic implementation.

When former athletes use conflict resolution skills in workplace situations, demonstrate cultural competence in diverse professional environments, apply systems thinking to business and community challenges, and maintain continuous learning orientations throughout their careers, they multiply the positive impact of their athletic experience far beyond any scoreboard outcome.

I get emails and phone calls from former athletes regularly. They tell me about using the G.R.A.C.E framework to resolve conflicts at work, about applying systems thinking to business decisions, about teaching their own children the principles they learned on our courts and fields.

A former soccer player who now manages a hospital emergency department wrote: "Every day I deal with high-stress situations where people are scared, angry, or in pain. The emotional regulation skills I learned playing for you—that's what helps me lead my team through chaos. You taught me that staying calm under pressure isn't weakness. It's leadership."

That's the ripple effect. That's what happens when you invest in character alongside competition.

BUILDING YOUR LEGACY

Victor's transformation from victim to advocate represents the ultimate potential of systematic culture development. The young man who nearly died from violence became an educator committed to preventing others from experiencing similar trauma. His master's program application described using athletic experiences to develop character competencies that now serve his professional effectiveness and community impact.

This is what systematic implementation creates: young people who are so positively influenced by their athletic experience that they want to share similar opportunities with others throughout their lives.

Your program's legacy isn't measured by championships alone. It's measured by the quality of people developed, the positive influence on community culture, and the lasting impact on everyone touched by your commitment to excellence in both performance and character.

REALITY CHECK

Successful implementation requires courage, patience, and persistence. You'll face resistance from people comfortable with toxic traditions. You'll encounter pressure to compromise character for short-term competitive advantage. You'll need determination when transformation takes longer than critics expect.

But you'll also discover that most stakeholders want programs that develop both excellence and character. You'll find unexpected allies and support. You'll experience the profound satisfaction that comes from knowing you're making a real difference in young people's lives that extends far beyond their athletic careers.

This work is hard. It will test you. There will be moments when reverting to old ways feels easier than continuing forward with new ones.

But remember: every time you choose character over convenience, you're building something that lasts. Every time you hold the line on principles when pressure says to compromise, you're modeling for young people what integrity looks like in real time.

The night Victor was stabbed, I stood in that hospital waiting room and wondered if I'd failed him. Years later, when Dr. Patterson called, I realized something different: We'd built something together that turned tragedy into transformation.

That's what this work does. It doesn't prevent every bad thing from happening. But it creates environments where people develop the skills and character to survive hard things, learn from them, and use them to make the world better.

Start today. Start small. Start with one principle, one conversation, one shift in how you respond to pressure.

Reflection Questions

1. **Implementation Readiness:** What specific evidence would indicate that your program is ready for comprehensive transformation, and what preliminary work might be needed?

2. **Resistance Management:** How would you handle situations where different stakeholder groups have conflicting expectations about program priorities and approaches?

3. **Resource Allocation:** Given your current constraints and competing demands, how would you prioritize which elements to implement first for maximum impact?

4. **Long-term Vision:** What would success look like for your program three years after systematic implementation, and how would you measure that success?

Chapter Assignment

Comprehensive Implementation Planning:
Create a detailed action plan for systematic culture development in your program:

Assessment and Planning:

- Complete comprehensive culture assessment using tools from Chapter 9
- Identify three highest-priority areas for immediate attention based on assessment results
- Analyze available resources, potential obstacles, and stakeholder readiness for change
- Develop realistic timeline for implementation that accounts for your specific context

90-Day Launch Plan:

- Design specific activities for each phase of initial implementation
- Create communication strategy for introducing changes to all stakeholder groups
- Establish measurement systems for tracking both competitive performance and character development
- Plan staff training and development needed for successful implementation

Long-term Sustainability Strategy:

- Identify potential culture carriers who can model and teach systematic principles
- Design policy integration that embeds character development into all program operations
- Create community partnership opportunities that reinforce and support program values
- Establish succession planning that maintains culture continuity during leadership transitions

Implementation and Evaluation:

- Begin immediate implementation of highest-priority elements while continuing comprehensive planning
- Document early results, challenges, and lessons learned for continuous improvement
- Adjust approaches based on stakeholder feedback and observed outcomes

- Plan expansion and refinement based on initial implementation experience

Chapter 13

Sustaining Change—
Building Legacy Programs

THE ULTIMATE VALIDATION

Victor graduated from college with an education degree and returned to Freedom as a teacher and assistant coach. "I want to bring these principles to a new generation of students," he told me during his interview.

I watched him walk into the building for that interview—the same building where he'd nearly died five years earlier. He moved through those hallways with purpose, not fear. He stopped to talk to students who were struggling, not because he was required to but because he understood what it meant to be seen when you feel invisible.

This is what sustainability looks like: young people who experienced something so positive they want to share it with others throughout their lives.

But Victor's return also taught me something else: sustainability isn't automatic. It requires deliberate systems, intentional planning, and constant vigilance against the forces that would pull programs back toward dysfunction.

During his first year back, Victor established a peer mediation program that taught middle school students the same conflict resolution skills he'd learned through athletics. He created mentoring relationships where high school athletes supported younger students facing academic and social challenges. He developed leadership opportunities that connected character development to community service.

Most significantly, he applied systematic approaches to prevent the kind of violence he had experienced. Victor understood that sustainable change requires more than just avoiding problems—it requires creating positive cultures where violence becomes unthinkable because people have developed better alternatives.

I'm going to use Victor's first three years back at Freedom as the framework for this chapter, because his journey illustrates everything you need to know about building programs that last beyond any individual leader.

FOUR WAYS YOUR CULTURE WILL COLLAPSE (IF YOU LET IT).

Leadership Transition

New coaches or administrators often want to impose their own methods rather than building on positive culture. They may view existing approaches as criticism of their previous experience or constraints on their leadership style. Without intentional succession planning, positive cultures can disappear when key supporters leave.

Competitive Pressure

When teams struggle, pressure to abandon

character-based approaches for "whatever works" can undermine years of culture development. Board members, parents, and community supporters may prioritize immediate results over long-term character development, especially during high-profile competitions or challenging seasons.

Cultural Drift

Without constant attention and reinforcement, even positive cultures tend to revert to previous patterns under stress. New participants join programs without understanding established values. Experienced members may become complacent about maintaining standards they previously fought to establish.

I watched it happen in real time. Younger athletes who hadn't experienced the old culture didn't understand why we did things differently. Senior athletes who remembered the transformation started slipping back into old habits when they felt pressure from the new athletic director.

Generational Turnover

As athletes graduate and new participants join, cultural knowledge gets diluted if transmission systems aren't intentionally designed and maintained. Stories that explain why certain approaches matter get lost. Relationships that reinforced positive behavior patterns end. New people may not understand the historical context that makes current practices meaningful.

This was the most insidious threat. Every year, we lost seniors who carried program history and gained freshmen who didn't know why things mattered. If we weren't deliberate about transferring knowledge, the culture would die one graduating class at a time.

DON'T JUST BUILD A PROGRAM – BUILD A PIPELINE

Sustainability requires infrastructure, not just inspiration.

Policy Integration

Sustainable programs embed character development into organizational systems rather than depending on individual commitment.

Revise hiring practice to include character competencies in job descriptions for all coaching positions. We assessed candidate alignment with program values alongside technical qualifications. We provided comprehensive orientation that included culture expectations and systematic training.

Embedded systematic principles in program handbooks, communication materials, and policy documents. Aligned budget priorities with culture development goals rather than treating character work as optional. Create recognition systems that celebrate both performance and character achievements equally.

"The values aren't negotiable. The methods can be. That distinction freedom within framework—is the key for sustainability. Create structures that protect non-negotiables while allowing adaptation.

WHO WILL CARRY THE FLAME?

By his second year, Victor had identified something crucial: we needed more people like him—.

Legacy programs develop multiple people who understand, model, and can teach program values to others. Cultural carriers, people who understood the culture deeply enough to protect and transmit it.

Identification and Development

Cultural carriers demonstrate systematic principles consistently, take initiative in supporting others' development, communicate program values effectively, show commitment to long-term success, and adapt applications to different situations while maintaining core values.

A formal training program for potential culture carriers:

- Advanced education in systematic principles and practical applications

- Leadership skills development including communication, conflict resolution, and mentoring abilities
- Understanding of adolescent development and positive youth development research
- Ongoing professional development opportunities

Succession Planning

Rather than depending on single individuals, build cultural carriers at multiple levels: head coaches, assistant coaches, senior athletes, experienced parents, alumni networks, and community supporters.

HOW TO PASS THE TORCH WITHOUT DROPPING IT

Documentation and Training

Written policies that clearly explained systematic principles and their applications. He developed training materials for new coaches that integrated character development with technical skill instruction. He designed orientation programs for new families that established expectations and provided education about program values.

Formal Mentoring Relationships

Establish partnerships between outgoing and

incoming leaders that include overlap periods for knowledge transfer. He paired experienced coaches with new staff members in both technical and character development approaches. He connected senior athletes with younger participants about program culture and leadership expectations.

"You can read about culture or you learn it by doing it with someone who already knows."

Institutional Memory Preservation

Conduct regular debriefing and reflection sessions that capture successful practices and lessons learned. Collect stories that preserve examples of transformation and character development for future inspiration. Maintain an alumni feedback system that documents long-term impact.

YOUR BIGGEST ENEMIES: EGO, DRIFT, AND THE BUDGET COMMITTEE

The threats to sustainability aren't abstract. They have names and faces and agendas.

Success Complacency

Programs that achieve initial positive results sometimes become complacent, assuming culture will maintain itself without continued attention and investment.

The football program has won championships two years running, and the coach started cutting corners on character development. "We're fine," "Look at our record."

Three months later, two star players were arrested for assault. The "fine" culture had been eroding while everyone focused on trophies.

Prevention: Treat culture development as an ongoing process rather than destination. Regular assessment even during successful periods. Recognition systems that celebrate cultural achievements alongside competitive success.

Drift During Difficulty

When the basketball team struggled, pressure mounted to abandon character-based approaches. Parents and other stakeholders may request coaching changes. Use your data to support and justify the actions of the coach to "Keep doing what we're doing". The character work is what will turn this around, if its not abandoned.

Prevention: Education about how character-based approaches enhance rather than inhibit competitive success. Support systems for leaders during difficult periods. Examples from other programs that maintained values during challenging circumstances.

Leadership Ego

Prevention: Clear communication about non-negotiable program values during hiring. Orientation processes that help new leaders understand existing culture before making changes. Community accountability that supports culture maintenance while allowing innovation.

Resource Constraints

Present data showing how positive culture reduces disciplinary incidents, improves retention, and increases community support that bring additional funding

Prevention: Integration of culture development into essential program operations. Demonstration of how positive culture reduces expenses through better retention and fewer problems. Documentation of benefits for resource allocation decisions.

WHAT LONG-TERM SUCCESS ACTUALLY LOOKS LIKE

Programs that successfully sustain systematic transformation over decades demonstrate specific characteristics that enable continuity through changing circumstances.

Victor helped me understand these not as abstract principles but as lived realities that either existed or didn't.

Values Clarity

Everyone can understand, explain, and apply program values to specific situations. Regular communication about values and their practical applications. Decision-making that consistently references values as primary criteria.

System Alignment

Policies, procedures, and practices consistently reinforce stated values. Recognition and accountability systems measure both performance and character equally. Resource allocation prioritizes culture development alongside competitive success.

"Show me what you celebrate," he said, "and I'll show you what you actually value."

Adaptive Capacity

Ability to adapt methods while maintaining core values. Learning from mistakes to strengthen culture. Innovation in systematic applications while preserving foundational principles. Balance between honoring tradition and embracing necessary change.

Methods changed. Values didn't.

Community Integration

Strong relationships with broader community based on shared values. Alumni networks that actively contribute to current program culture. Partnerships with other organizations that reinforce positive youth development. Recognition from the community for program contributions beyond athletic achievement.

"Culture doesn't stop at the gymnasium door, we need the whole community carrying the same message."

ARE WE STILL ON TRACK?

Leading Indicators (predict whether change will continue)

Number of staff trained in systematic approaches. Quality of mentoring relationships between experienced and new participants. Community engagement in culture education and support. Integration of character indicators in evaluation and recognition systems.

Every quarter, review these indicators. Not to judge or punish, but to identify drift early enough to correct it.

Lagging Indicators (show whether efforts are succeeding)

Culture consistency during leadership transitions and challenging circumstances. Program reputation over time as measured by stakeholder satisfaction. Alumni feedback about lasting impact.

YOUR SUSTAINABILITY ACTION PLAN

Year 1: Foundation Building

- Document current successful practices and lessons learned
- Identify and begin developing cultural carriers at all program levels
- Integrate systematic principles into essential program operations and policy documents
- Begin building community understanding and support

Year 2: System Integration

- Embed culture indicators into all evaluation and recognition systems
- Develop comprehensive training programs for new participants and staff
- Create alumni network and community partnership systems
- Establish regular assessment and improvement processes

Year 3: Expansion and Refinement

- Mentor other programs seeking to implement systematic approaches
- Refine and improve practices based on experience and feedback
- Strengthen community partnerships and support systems
- Document and share sustainability lessons learned

Years 4+: Legacy Development

- Maintain culture excellence through multiple leadership transitions
- Continue contributing to broader knowledge about sustainable positive athletic culture
- Develop next generation of leaders across all stakeholder groups
- Expand influence to support character development in other youth-serving organizations

---

REALITY CHECK

Sustainability requires different skills than initial implementation. Starting systematic approaches demands vision, courage, and persistence during resistance and skepticism. Maintaining them over time requires patience, adaptability, and commitment to continuous improvement while preserving core values.

The most sustainable programs are those that understand culture development as ongoing investment rather than one-time achievement. They celebrate progress while acknowledging continued growth opportunities. They honor tradition while embracing innovation. They maintain consistency while adapting to changing circumstances.

Build your pipeline. Train your culture carriers. Document your systems. Create your redundancies.

But most importantly, remember why it matters. Because somewhere in your program right now is a student like Victor—someone whose life might depend on the culture you're building and protecting.

Reflection Questions

1. **Sustainability Readiness:** What evidence would indicate that your program culture could survive leadership transitions and challenging circumstances?

2. **Cultural Carrier Development:** How would you identify and develop multiple people capable of maintaining positive change throughout your program and community?

3. **System Integration:** What would need to change for character development to be embedded in all program operations rather than treated as an additional requirement?

4. **Legacy Impact:** What evidence would demonstrate your program's lasting influence on participants' lives and broader community culture?

Chapter Assignment

Legacy Program Development Plan: Create a comprehensive strategy for sustaining systematic culture development over time:

Current Sustainability Assessment:

- Evaluate your program's current capacity for maintaining positive culture through challenges and transitions
- Identify potential cultural carriers among athletes, coaches, parents, and community members
- Analyze systems that would need modification to embed character development permanently
- Assess community relationships and support systems that contribute to program sustainability

Cultural Carrier Development Strategy:

- Design identification and training programs for potential culture carriers at multiple levels
- Create mentoring relationships that transfer knowledge and commitment from experienced to emerging leaders
- Establish succession planning that maintains culture continuity during predictable transitions
- Build alumni networks that provide ongoing support and accountability for current program leadership

System Integration Plan:

- Develop policy modifications that embed systematic principles in all program operations
- Create evaluation and recognition systems that measure character development alongside competitive performance
- Design training programs for new staff and participants that integrate culture development with skill instruction
- Establish community partnerships that reinforce and support program values beyond athletic activities

Long-term Impact Strategy:

- Create measurement systems that track long-term influence of program participation on character development and life success
- Develop documentation approaches that preserve institutional knowledge and successful practices
- Design community engagement strategies that expand positive influence beyond immediate program participants
- Establish research and evaluation partnerships that contribute to broader knowledge about character development through athletics

Implement highest-priority elements immediately while developing comprehensive long-term sustainability systems.

Conclusion: Your Choice, Your Legacy

LEGACY IS BUILT IN DAILY DECISIONS

In practices and games, in conversations and conflicts, in moments of victory and defeat, athletic leaders make choices that shape young people's futures. These choices either perpetuate harmful patterns or create positive change that lasts for generations.

You can accept toxic traditions because "that's how it's always been done." You can measure success solely by scoreboards while ignoring human cost. You can maintain the status quo that drives 70% of kids out of sports by age 13[37].

Or you can choose transformation.

You can implement evidence-based approaches that develop both champions and citizens. You can create environments where young people thrive rather than merely survive competitive pressure. You can build programs that communities take pride in for generations because they represent the best of what athletics can accomplish.

Every time you respond to a mistake with curiosity instead of criticism, you're choosing transformation.

Every time you celebrate an athlete's character growth alongside their performance improvement, you're choosing transformation.

Every time you hold the line on values when pressure says to compromise, you're choosing transformation.

Every time you model respect when officials make questionable calls, you're choosing transformation.

Every time you address conflicts through problem-solving instead of punishment, you're choosing transformation.

Legacy isn't built in championship moments. It's built in Tuesday afternoon practices when nobody's watching, in halftime conversations when emotions are high, in parking lot interactions with frustrated parents, in quiet conversations with struggling athletes who need to know their worth isn't measured by playing time.

Legacy is built in daily decisions that either align with your stated values or expose them as empty words.

CHARACTER VS. COMPETITION IS A FALSE CHOICE

I've heard it a thousand times: "We can't focus on character and still be competitive. We have to choose."

That's a lie. And the research proves it.

UCLA's John Wooden won 10 NCAA championships in 12 years using character-based coaching principles. Research consistently shows that programs implementing systematic approaches to character development often achieve both competitive success and higher satisfaction rates among all participants[38].

The highest-performing programs excel at both character development and competitive success. Not one or the other. Both.

The real choice is between sustainable excellence that develops people alongside performance, and unsustainable toxicity that burns through talented individuals while creating community damage that extends far beyond athletics.

Programs that prioritize character don't sacrifice competitive edge—they enhance it. Athletes who feel psychologically safe take appropriate risks that lead to breakthrough performances. Teams with positive chemistry execute better under pressure. Players who trust their coaches perform better when it matters most.

Character-based approaches create competitive advantage, not competitive disadvantage.

The programs that struggle aren't the ones that prioritize character too much. They're the ones that prioritize winning so exclusively that they destroy the team chemistry, psychological safety, and trust that enable winning in the first place.

Stop choosing between character and competition. Start building both through systematic, intentional culture development that makes excellence and integrity partners instead of opponents.

NEVER AGAIN, ON PURPOSE

Fifteen years ago, I knelt beside a bleeding seventeen-year-old and vowed such violence would never happen again in programs under my influence.

The night Victor was stabbed, I thought my career was over. I thought I'd failed at the most fundamental responsibility—keeping students safe. I stood in that hospital waiting room and wondered how I'd missed the signs, ignored the warnings, allowed culture to deteriorate so badly that violence felt like a reasonable response to conflict.

"Never again" doesn't happen by accident. It happens on purpose, through systematic implementation of principles that create cultures where violence becomes unthinkable because people have developed better alternatives.

It happens because leaders like you choose to build something better than what exists.

YOUR LEGACY STARTS TODAY

The research is clear: positive athletic experiences

that prioritize both excellence and character development produce better competitive results and better human beings. The strategies exist, the evidence supports them, and the tools are available through the G.R.A.C.E framework.

Everything you need to begin systematic culture transformation is in this book:

- Assessment tools that reveal current culture accurately
- The G.R.A.C.E framework that creates positive change systematically
- Measurement approaches that track both performance and character development
- Sustainability strategies that ensure continuity through challenges and transitions

The research supports character-based approaches to athletic excellence. The examples prove they work in real programs with real challenges. The community needs leaders willing to demonstrate that competition can develop rather than destroy character in young people.

This Week: Assess current culture honestly using the tools provided throughout this book. Identify one principle to focus on first based on your program's specific needs and challenges. Don't try to change everything. Just start.

This Month: Train key staff in systematic approaches. Establish feedback systems that track culture alongside performance. Begin measuring both competitive outcomes and character development indicators. Make this work visible and valued.

This Season: Implement systematic approaches consistently across all program activities. Address resistance through education and persistence. Document what works for continuous improvement and community sharing. Build momentum through small wins.

This Year: Build sustainability systems that ensure positive culture continues regardless of leadership changes, competitive pressures, or community challenges. Develop internal expertise that can maintain and expand character development work over time. Create infrastructure that outlasts you.

Leading positive change requires tremendous courage. You'll face resistance from people comfortable with toxic traditions that feel familiar even when they're harmful. You'll encounter pressure to compromise character for short-term competitive advantage. You'll need persistence when transformation takes longer than skeptics expect.

But you'll also discover that most people—athletes, parents, community members—want programs that develop both excellence and character. You'll find unexpected allies in places you didn't anticipate. You'll experience the profound satisfaction that comes from knowing you're making a real difference in young people's lives that extends far beyond any scoreboard or trophy case.

The young people in your program deserve more than just technical instruction and competitive opportunities. They deserve environments that develop their potential as athletes and human beings. They need adults who understand that their worth transcends their performance and that their character development serves their long-term success more than any championship they might win.

Your community watches your choices and learns about values through the athletic programs you create and maintain. Your legacy gets written in every decision about how competition and character development can strengthen rather than compete with each other.

The opportunity to make a lasting positive difference is available right now, in your program, with your current athletes and families. The G.R.A.C.E framework provides the roadmap. The research validates the approach. The tools enable implementation.

The only question remaining is whether you have the courage to choose transformation over tradition, systematic development over hope and chance, and legacy impact over short-term results.

The question tht drives me: Why would anyone choose toxic culture when healthy culture exists and can be restored. What I have learned, isthat many people don't realize they have a choice. They accept dysfunction as inevitable because it's what they've always experienced. They tolerate disrespect because they think that's what competition requires.

Leading with G.R.A.C.E demonstrates that we can choose different

About the Author

Alva L. Amaker, M.Ed, CAA, CCT, is CEO and Founder of A&A Athletic Consulting, Vigilance Safety Training Center, DCPG Sports, and the Etiquette Excellence Academy. With over 30 years of experience spanning K–12, collegiate, and community sports, she is a Certified Health Educator and Certified Athletic Administrator known for developing impactful athletic programs, building student leadership boards, and creating safety-first systems for events and sports environments. She is also a Certified Civility Trainer, and a Certified AI Consultant.

Since 1994, Alva has delivered first responder and safety training across the U.S. and was honored by Civility Worldwide for her leadership in promoting emotionally grounded sports cultures. She holds a B.S. in Health and Physical Education from Central State University and an M.Ed. in Organizational Leadership from American Intercontinental University. She also earned advanced credentials from the University of Southern Mississippi's National Center for Spectator Sports Safety and Security (NCS4), and FEMA.

Alva is a proud member of the National Interscholastic Athletic Administrators Association (NIAAA), NOMAD, WISE, and several national safety and sports leadership organizations. She co-hosts the podcast *Pandora's Playbook* and is currently building the Vigilant Safety Solution app, which supports player safety and event management.

The transformative night described in this book when seventeen-year-old Victor Thompson was stabbed at a high school volleyball game—changed the trajectory of her career and led to the development of the G.R.A.C.E framework. Since then, she has dedicated her professional life to developing practical approaches to character development through athletics, working with hundreds of programs to implement evidence-based culture change that serves both competitive excellence and human development.

This book represents not just professional expertise, but personal mission born from crisis and sustained by hope that every young athlete deserves better than what previous generations accepted as inevitable. Victor's transformation from victim to advocate—returning to Freedom High School as a teacher and coach, validates years of systematic work to create athletic environments where violence becomes unthinkable because communities have built something better.

Leading with G.R.A.C.E: Building Civil Sports Communities provides practical tools for athletic leaders who understand that their responsibility extends beyond scoreboards to include the character development of young people who will shape communities for generations to come.

Citations and References

[1] U.S. Center for SafeSport. (2019). "SafeSport Research: Understanding and Preventing Abuse in Sport."

[2] National Association of Sports Officials. (2020). "2020 Officiating Survey Report."

[3] Aspen Institute Project Play. (2019). "State of Play 2019: Trends and Developments in Youth Sports."

[4] NCAA Sport Science Institute. (2016). "Mental Health Best Practices: Inter-Association Consensus Document."

[5] National Association of Sports Officials. (2019). "Sports Officiating: A Profession Under Siege."

[6] Ibid.

[7] Associated Press. (2022, June 5). "Youth baseball coach arrested for punching 72-year-old umpire in New Jersey."

[8] Aspen Institute Project Play. (2024). "State of Play 2024: Trends and Developments in Youth Sports."

[9] Vertommen, T., et al. (2023). "Interpersonal violence experiences of young elite athletes: Prevalence and correlates of four types of violence in six European countries." *PMC Research Study*.

[10] Various news reports compiled from Associated

Press, Reuters, and local news sources, 2024.

[11] Institut national de santé publique du Québec. (2023). "Violence in Youth Sports: A Comprehensive Study."

[12] Stankovich, C. (2023, August). "Youth Sports Violence Trends: 20-Year Analysis." *Sports Psychology Today*.

[13] European Games Athletic Performance Study. (2019). "Cortisol and Athletic Performance: Track and Field Analysis."

[14] Performance Psychology Research Institute. (2020). "Chronic Stress Impact on Athletic Decision-Making."

[15] Olympic Historical Archives. (1936). "Jesse Owens and Luz Long: Friendship Beyond Competition."

[16] Horn, T.S. (2008). "Coaching effectiveness research: A meta-analysis of coaching behaviors." *Journal of Sport and Exercise Psychology*.

[17] National Association of Sports Officials. (2020). "2020 Officiating Survey Report."

[18] Gould, D., et al. (2008). "The role of parents in tennis success: Focus group interviews with junior coaches." *The Sport Psychologist*, 22(1), 18-37.

[19] NCAA Research Department. (2023). "College

Athletic Scholarship Statistics."

[20] Gottman, J.M. (1994). "What Predicts Relationship Success: The 5:1 Ratio." *Journal of Marriage and Family Therapy*.

[21] Bandura, A. (1977). *Social Learning Theory*. Englewood Cliffs, NJ: Prentice Hall.

[22] MIT Technology Review. (2023). "Why negative news spreads faster on social media platforms."

[23] ESPN Legal Analysis. (2024). "Youth Sports Settlement Database: Legal Costs and Trends."

[24] Aspen Institute Project Play. (2019). "State of Play 2019: Trends and Developments in Youth Sports."

[25] Youth Sports Research Institute. (2022). "Retention Rates in Positive Culture Athletic Programs."

[26] Positive Coaching Alliance. (2023). "Program Growth Through Referral Marketing Study."

[27] Performance Psychology Research Institute. (2020). "Chronic Stress Impact on Athletic Decision-Making."

[28] Positive Coaching Alliance. (2024). "20-Year Impact Report: Reaching 19.2 Million Youth."

[29] Rohleder, N., et al. (2006). "The psychosocial

stress-induced increase in salivary alpha-amylase." *Psychophysiology*, 43(6), 645-652.

[30] Hedstrom, R., & Gould, D. (2004). "Research in youth sports: Critical issues status." Institute for the Study of Youth Sports, Michigan State University.

[31] Center for Creative Leadership. (2019). "Behavioral Change Timeline: Research on Habit Formation in Organizational Settings."

[32] McKinsey & Company. (2020). "Culture and Performance: The Business Case for Culture Development."

[33] Wooden, J., & Jamison, S. (2005). *Wooden on Leadership: How to Create a Winning Organization*.

[34] National Parent Teacher Association. (2023). "Parent Priorities in Child Development Survey."

[35] Fraser-Thomas, J.L., et al. (2005). "Youth sport programs: An avenue to foster positive youth development." *Physical Education & Sport Pedagogy*, 10(1), 19-40.

[36] Search Institute. (2020). "Developmental Assets Framework: 40 Research-Based Assets for Positive Youth Development."

[37] Aspen Institute Project Play. (2019). "State of Play 2019: Trends and Developments in Youth Sports."

[38] Danish, S.J., et al. (2004). "Enhancing youth development through sport." *World Leisure Journal*, 46(3), 38-49.

Leading with G.R.A.C.E: Building Civil Sports Communities provides the roadmap for creating athletic environments where competition serves character development, where mistakes become learning opportunities, and where young people develop into better human beings through sport. The choice is yours. The time is now.

www.ingramcontent.com/pod-product-compliance
Lightning Source LLC
Chambersburg PA
CBHW052051220426
43663CB00012B/2522